MAKE IT
MATTER
that you're here

K. Hart

Make It Matter That You're Here

1st Edition: June, 2016

Scripture quotations Copyright © 2016, NIV; NKJV; and MSG versions of the Bible.

Cover Design by Kirsten Hart

Interior Design by Kirsten Hart Copyright © 2016 Author Name

ISBN: 1519293186
ISBN-13: 9781519293183

DEDICATION

I honestly need to dedicate this book to all of the high schoolers I have been able to hang out with for the past thirteen years of working in high schools. Yes, Mrs. Hart has been a simple and lowly 'sub' in-between speaking and singing engagements and 'gigs', but my gosh I have loved every day. You guys make me *laugh,* and I honestly like you more than most adults in this world (don't tell them I said that).

CONTENTS

HOW TO USE THIS BOOK

The last thing I want for a junior high or high school student to have is additional stress from having to read this book. I don't have any fill-in-the-blank questions, and I don't want anyone to get in trouble if they aren't caught up on their chapter readings. It's *just* a book. But I *would* love for you to get as much as you can from reading this, and going through the questions in the back. Answer the questions on your own, or in youth group, or small group. Whichever you prefer, or your youth pastor prefers.

But please know...if you *fall asleep reading my book*? I'll know. Trust me. And my feelings will be incredibly hurt.

Peace out.

MATTERING

From the beginning of time, people have been searching for the reason they are here. It's not a new question. It's not a newer way of thinking. Every single human being born has wondered "what am I here to accomplish?" I think about it almost daily. Why was I born *when* I was born? Who would I be if I had been born in the Middle Ages? Would I still have been *me*? What is my purpose? What was I born to accomplish? Does it actually matter that I exist?

My personal beliefs? I absolutely believe that there is a reason and purpose to why and when we were born. King David mentions in Psalm 139 that "all the days ordained for me were written in your book before one of them came to be." I believe that God inspired David to write those words.

And I believe they are true. Do you? Do you know that before you were even born that every day of your life was ordained or ordered?

In my mind, it's hard for me to wrap my mind around the thought that every single human being that has been born since the creation of man was planned by God, and that before they even took their first breath, God knew each and every one of their 'days'. I'm certainly not a mathematician, but I know a *lot* of people have come and gone before you and I came along. To use a very juvenile word, there have been *bazillions*.

Is each life supposed to make a difference, or is it planned for some to purely just exist? What about those born in far-off remote countries that never left the same village all of their ancestors lived and died in? Or people born on remote islands in the middle of the ocean. Are those lives less important than ours born in this era of entrepreneurs with medical and scientific advances? Are we to make more of a difference in this world, because we come from an advanced country and society?

Some of you reading this might think it unfair that you were born into your family. Perhaps you have experienced emotional or physical abuse, and wonder why God placed you with your set of parents. Couldn't God have loved you more, and given you a family where love, not anger, was the most common emotion? If he knew every day of your life, why did he chose to give you an abusive home? Can God still use you with all the junk you have experienced in your life? Are you worthy of being used for good in this world?

Maybe you are the only one in your family with a desire to go to church, and study about God and Jesus. Why did he place in you a home that has different beliefs than what you feel inside? Do you feel as if you are in this whole Christianity thing alone with zero support from your family?

I grew up in a Christian household. Both of my parents led the music at churches that I was raised in. I had a solid foundation in the church, and biblical beliefs. Yet here I am, a grown woman, still wondering if I'm actually making a difference in this world, and '*mattering*'. If I know one thing for sure, it's that I still have so much to learn. My knowledge of God and how he works is still so elementary. He is so vast, and we are so small. Yet he chooses to speak and work *through* us? How can that be? When we make wrong choices and bad decisions, he still loves us, and desires to change the world through our very actions and words. It's hard to fathom.

I respect who you are and your age. I don't want to talk down to you in this book, but rather treat you as an equal. Let's journey through this book together. Even though I'm not sitting there with you, know that my mind is with you as we both still grow and discover through this book.

If you meet an adult that says they have it all together—move on to someone else. Not that we can't have knowledge and learned skills and understanding, but we are all on the same road of discovering who we are in God, and what our ultimate purpose is. Each and every day is a learning opportunity. The wisest people know that they have so much more to learn.

My hope is that by the end of this book, you will have a clearer insight into your giftings, and how God desires to use *you* in your lifetime. Your days are limited. I don't mean to be a Debbie Downer with that announcement, but it's true. We only have so many years, months, and days to inhabit this Earth. Let's make them count. Let's discover early on what we are meant to accomplish while each of us is here.

God has ordained you for greatness, but often our interpretation of something great is far different from what God has in mind. What if you were born to help only one person? If everything in your life, all of your training, schooling, and experience was only to assist and make the difference for one singular person, would it be worth it all?

When I was forty-one, I accidentally discovered that I had been adopted. My parents never told me, and I never had the slightest thought that I wasn't born to both of them. I had to find my birth certificate to get a new passport for a trip we were to take. I couldn't find my birth certificate anywhere.

Ordering a copy of my certificate online, opened up a whole new completely unexpected world. Through the state of New York searching for my certificate, I learned that I was not who I always thought I was. My life was turned upside down. I had no idea that I was adopted. You know how some people will say, 'There's no way I belong in this family, I'm so opposite', or they feel that they don't look like anyone else in the family? Complete opposite with me. I looked like my mom. I totally fit in with the family.

After months and months of searching for the truth, I was able to discover the adoption agency that adopted me out. I received paperwork from them about my birth mother. They weren't able to give me any specific identification about her, but there were still five pages of details. I was reading through this letter that told me what she looked like, and what her sisters and brother were like. Then I read a sentence that changed my life.

It read, "In the Fall of 1965, your mother and her mother (my grandma!) had all the connections and money they needed, and flew to Sweden to obtain an abortion. After being in Sweden for a month, they weren't able to find anyone that would perform the abortion, and they came back to the United States". I was supposed to have been aborted in Sweden? I'm not supposed to be alive?

Sometimes your life can change in an instant. Mine did. Finding out that I wasn't even supposed to be alive changed my life. I had a new story. My boring life instantly became an unreal story. And I felt I needed to share that story.

A few years ago, I was invited to speak for a ladies Christmas Tea. I shared about my adoption discovery, and tied it into the Christmas theme of 'Unexpected Gifts'. Two weeks later, I received an email from a woman who attended that tea.

In this email, she told me that there had been a woman that sat at her table that she didn't know very well (let's call this woman Abby), and who wasn't a regular attender at their church. Two weeks after Abby sat and heard me speak, she found out that her sixteen year-old daughter was pregnant. Apparently Abby had forced another daughter of hers to have an abortion. Abby mentioned that because she heard my story, they were going to keep this baby, and not abort it.

If my whole crazy discovery about being adopted was only for this one unborn baby, it was all worth it. My story had made the difference between life and death of a baby in the womb. To me, that is life changing. Did the whole world hear what happened because of me telling my story that day? No. But the whole world didn't matter. As long as Abby heard those words.

Perhaps your life's purpose is to make a difference in the lives of only a few. But you never know what could come from those few you touch. The reason I'm writing this book is to let you know, whether to a few, or to millions, you can change lives for the better.

I thought my adoption story would be something I'd share primarily to women's groups, but the doors have opened to share it for many church services. At least two separate times after I shared my story, I had grown men come up and want to talk with me. Each man secretly shared that they had fathered children, but never got in contact with their babies. One man said his daughter was in her late twenties. Each said that after hearing me share my story, they wanted to search out their children.

Again, perhaps it was only *two* men that were inspired to search for their children. But what about those children they want to search for, and their spouses, and *their* children. Just because you only *see* one or two people that are changed because of you, doesn't mean that there aren't tons more that are associated with those one or two. It's the ripple effect.

If you haven't studied the ripple effect in science classes, you will. Its definition is: a spreading effect or series of consequences caused by a single action or event. *You* can cause a ripple effect for others by reaching out and making a difference. Never think your life is insignificant because you don't seem to be changing the world in record time. It happens one person at a time. Unless you get crazy famous. Which you could. That would be really cool.

To make it matter that you're in this world, you need to know what your purpose is. What makes you unique? What your calling is. What your dreams are, and how you find that out.

OLD SCHOOL

The nights were short. The days were long. You worked all day for a few dollars. You could hardly put enough food on the table to feed your family. And, yes, you had to walk ten miles in the snow to school barefoot, and it was uphill both ways.

I thoroughly realize that life was a lot harder 'back in the day'. I, for one, am so thankful that I wasn't born in a time when outdoor toilets were still being used. I am thankful for inside facilities. Very. Although I have heard of areas that still had outhouses in use within the past ten years. Unbelievable.

You go to school, finish high school if you're lucky, get a job, get married, have some kids, work until retirement age, and retire to Florida. You were grateful to have had a job. It was work. Lots of hard work for little pay. Suck it up, and be thankful.

That was life. Some people were fortunate enough to have *careers*. Those were the rich people. Doctors, Judges, Professional Athletes, College Professors, all of those in the medical field and in politics were career people. Careers were prestigious. Jobs were commonplace. Then there were those people called actors.

The actors in Hollywood were the lucky ones. They got paid the big bucks to 'play' all day. They went to big Hollywood parties. What a life. Living in Beverly Hills and enjoying all the niceties life had to offer. That kind of lifestyle was only reserved for the elite. Just a few. The rest of the world trudged through jobs. Many in factory jobs. The only goal was to receive that paycheck at the end of the week. A position in management was sometimes the only goal, but those positions were reserved for the young up-and-coming kids.

I started my job career young. I was a Brownie selling Girl Scout Cookies. My parents were teaching music at a private college prep school in Princeton, New Jersey. We, as well as most of the school staff, lived on the grounds. Such a beautiful place. My family lived in a staff apartment in the grand Russell Hall building, which was a huge family estate mansion house turned dormitory for the all-boys boarding school. Very Ivy League. Very high-brow East Coast.

I was given the daunting task, as so many before me and so many after me have had, of selling Girl Scout Cookies. This was in the early 1970's. Back when just the basic cookies were available. Back when you got a decent amount of Thin Mints in your box! Two large sleeves to be exact! Heaven in a plastic sleeve. And, oh, Thin Mints straight out of the freezer...nothing better!

Back to my selling story. Well, I was on a mission. Sell, sell, sell! There were only a few times a day when a *girl* would be allowed to enter the boy's dorms. When that hour arrived, I entered. And I sold. I knocked on every single dorm room door of every single dorm. Those rich high school boys *ordered* my cookies! They ordered so many boxes that I was the #1 seller for that season. Thank you. Thank you very much. I think I won a ribbon or something. A ribbon and the knowledge that I had beat out every other Brownie in my troupe for the #1 spot.

That next fall, my Johnson Park Elementary School had a fund raising campaign. The campaign involved selling pre-printed Christmas cards. Trust me, they were all the rage in the early 70's. Very vogue. Basically they were Christmas cards that you could have your name, the names of all your family members, and whatever special Christmas greeting you wanted professionally printed at the bottom of the MERRY CHRISTMAS generic page. This time I had an even better selling incentive. PRIZES! And *good* prizes, mind you. Look OUT Hun School!

This time I not only hit up all the employees, staff, and teachers at the Hun School, I also canvassed every single residence in the neighborhood. My borders were the two busy streets: Lawrenceville Road and Rosedale Road. The streets and houses in-between? All my selling territory!

I had my catalog in hand and set out. Ding-Dong. Knock-Knock. I knew these houses from Trick-or-Treating, but now I would know them in a whole new way. These were the people who would help me get those PRIZES!

I sold. And I sold. And I sold. That's right. #1 seller AGAIN, thank you very much! (As I'm writing this I'm wondering why I went into a career of singing, speaking, and writing instead of SALES...) I don't recall how many boxes of Christmas cards I sold that year, but I do remember it took me days to get them all delivered. My little, 'Hello, my name is Kirsten...' speech that I gave to open the deal making worked well.

I got some serious prize loot, too. I bought a new blender for my parents (Did they suggest that I pick that item??? My memory is failing me), a rock tumbler (very, very 1970's), jewelry making kits, and literally box loads of fun stuff! The business woman in me was born.

My parents picked up on my door-to-door selling 'giftedness'. Not too long after my Christmas card sell-a-thon, they thought to capitalize on this new selling machine of theirs. I was no longer just their child. My childhood innocence and days of playing with Barbies was gone. It was time to get out and earn my keep. I was now the newest TOILET BOWL CLEANER saleswoman in town. Yep. You read that right.

My parents bought cases of these hook-on-the-back-of-the-inside-of-your-toilet-tank blue dye cleaners. Just the perfect fit for a little 8 year-old girl to sell. 'She sold the heck out of those Christmas cards, I'm thinking this girl could sell toilet bowl cleaners like nobody's business'. My parents wrote my sales pitch on a 3 x 5 index card. "Take this and memorize it", I was told. This wasn't seeming as fun as a selling Christmas cards that had a whole brochure full of prizes you could win. My parents handed me no such potential prize list. No rock tumbling or jewelry making kits as incentives. Just an index card. An index card with a lot of words on it to memorize.

I was a good girl. I memorized my pitch. I adjusted the right inflections for certain words that my parents coached me with. "Now go to our front door and pretend we are someone you are giving the pitch to". When I had the "Hello, my name is..." speech down pat, I was off. I had a whole case of toilet bowl cleaners to sell that afternoon, with more sitting in our basement.

I guess something about my "Please buy these strange objects from me" look worked. It worked well enough that after the cases of toilet bowl cleaners were sold, my parents thought I was ready for an upgrade. I was upgraded from inside the tank toilet bowl cleaners to sit-on-top-of-the-tank-lid glass domed plastic flower-filled room fresheners. If your parents lived in the 70's they will probably remember these. On the road a few years ago, when staying in a host home, I almost fainted when I saw one of MY glass flowered room fresheners sitting on TOP OF THEIR TOILET! Just how many years had that thing been sitting there? Unbelievable.

If I remember correctly, these fancy fresheners were available in three scents, and multiple plastic flower-colored looks.

They had vitamin E looking capsules in the bottom, that you would prick with a pin to make the scent come out stronger. These were a little harder to tote door-to-door than the toilet tank cleaners. I was a little girl working with glass containers. Really mom and dad? *Really*?

I received a new 3 x 5 with yet another sales pitch to memorize. Once again, I went outside of our front door and worked the speech with my parents, who for all acting and selling purposes weren't my 'parents', but rather neighbors who were potential customers. When I got the thumbs up that I was prepared enough to hit the neighborhood, I was a selling machine. I'm thinking at this point the neighbors were being sweet, and participating in 'pity buys'. "Maybe if we buy enough of these bathroom fresheners, this poor little girl won't be sent out anymore."

After I hit up every neighbor within walking distance, my parents got the genius idea to expand my territory. "We're going to drop you off here, and we'll pick you up again in two hours." It was just me and two cases of plastic flowered fresheners. A new neighborhood. New people. New bathrooms that needed to be scented. I just wanted to be home eating some cookies and playing with my Barbie pop-up camper and jeep.

I am seriously amazed that I wasn't abducted during those months. I know there wasn't as much talk of abductions in those days, but honestly, I was just a little girl! A little girl walking around with glass and plastic flowered bathroom deodorizers and a manila envelope filled with cash. I'm thinking I may need some therapy right now. Anyone available? Text me your number.

The awful thing is, I don't recall keeping much of the toilet bowl cleaner or bathroom-scenter money? I suppose it went towards clothes and food! I 'earned my keep' in those days. See, I know what hard work is! Perhaps I didn't have to slave away in coal mines, but for goodness sake, I was a young girl peddling my wares around foreign neighborhoods! And for additional pity emphasis, I played the cello in fourth and fifth grade, and I walked over a mile to and from school carrying that huge instrument! Pity? Any pity votes coming my way?

Eventually the toilet and bathroom products were all sold, and my first 'real' job was working in the cafeteria at my high school. I was what they called a 'day student', while most of the people attending The Pennington School were boarders. Again, very east coast. On Saturdays, I worked in the cafeteria for breakfast, lunch, and dinner. I think I made probably $35 a

Saturday, which was nice extra money that I kept for myself this time.

The goal of an actual career lay ahead of me. If I went to college and studied hard, I could make money doing what I loved. I was given a different school of thought than the generations before me. Times had changed!

Today gobs of professional athletes are paid outrageous salaries for 'playing' their sports. The billionaires of today are those who have come up with original ideas, marketed those ideas, and enjoy what they do. 'Find a problem and solve it' is the key to success. The people who sat and tinkered for fun in their garages are turning those creations into the world's greatest money makers. Life isn't all about all work and no play. Video game designers play all day, and get paid millions of dollars to do so!

It's a whole new world, my friends. You are just one creative and innovative thought away from being a millionaire. Seriously! Isn't that exciting?

I've always been searching for my possible million dollar idea. And I've had a few. My best? Why, that would be Meal Scented Candles! You'll be wishing you had been the first one to come up with this fantastic idea. Trust me. It's pure genius.

Now here's how I thought up the candle idea. I walked into our home one afternoon when a roast was cooking in the crock pot. Is that not just one of the best smells in the world? Agree with me here. It's comforting, it makes a house smell like a home, and the anticipation of a wonderful meal awaiting you is second to none. Now, who wouldn't want to reproduce that intoxicating scent anytime they wanted?

My mind started racing. Lasagna scented, chicken soup scented, BBQ scented, Thanksgiving dinner scented, and the list went on! What if I divided the candles into three separate sections? Say, perhaps for the Thanksgiving Meal Candle, I have one section that smelled like turkey basting another that smelled like sweet potato casserole and a third that replicated homemade yeast rolls. I bet you're getting hungry just reading this! See...great idea, huh!

"Dave," I called to my husband, "I totally have our money making idea! Oprah is so going to have this on her Favorite Things show next year!"

I got brainstorming. I could market these candles to anyone, but especially bachelors and non-cookers. What bachelor wouldn't want to bring home a date with his house smelling like a fresh baked Italian dinner, and then pull out a Stouffer's lasagna out of the oven? It would smell like he had been baking all day (especially with the Lasagna/Garlic Bread/Fettuccine Trio Candle burning). The ideas were flowing non-stop. Yeah, this was great money making stuff. And believe me, from my days of going door-to-door, I could spot a good money maker a mile away.

I brainstormed as any good inventor does. I wrote down on paper my brilliant trio candle scents. No more debt for this family. Trips, new cars, and large houses lay in wait for our future. This was *it*.

It was getting late in the evening, but my mind. was racing. It was time to make my test product. Time to create my baby. It was as if I were Dr. Frankenstein (which, if you recall, was actually the name of the scientist in the movie who created the monster, not the name of the monster) and I was about to bring life to this new creature of mine. Muwaa-haa-haa-haaa (evil laugh). Time to run to Walmart for supplies.

Michael's and Hobby Lobby were my first choices for meal scented candle making supplies, but at this time of night, they were both closed already. Walmart it was. 11pm and I was on my way. Craziness, I know, but when an idea is birthing inside of you, you need to seize the moment! Take note.

The last time I had created a candle was in Mrs. Papp's 4th grade class at Lore

Elementary. We were studying the American Revolutionary War, and a special guest came into our classroom to teach us the fine art of candle making. Mrs. Papp would be proud of me (God rest her soul, if she's even still alive after all these years) that I was attempting to relive that candle making experience. If I recall correctly, I believe the woman who taught us to 'dip...now dip again...and again...' was wearing Revolutionary War appropriate clothing. Some of the reenactors take that stuff way too seriously.

What did I need? Glass jars. Check. String. Check. A pencil to tie the string to at the top of the jar. Check. Now wax. No wax chips in the craft section at this Walmart. Hobby Lobby would have made this all the much easier. Dang. I put my thinking cap on and headed to the candles section. I found some unscented white candle tapers. Perfect. Well, perfect enough for the experiment for tonight. I would have to order wax chips in bulk for the future. Did they sell them that way? I would search that out in the morning.

Now for the first of my scents. Which meal did I want to recreate for my first (of many) Meal Candles. Drum roll, please. Actually, it was getting close to midnight, and Dr. Frankenstein-a was starting to get sleepy. Let's get on with this...

I went to the spices aisle. I looked at what

they had. It was time for the genius to kick in. What meal could I reproduce from these spices in front of me? I saw the chicken bouillon cubes. A·ha. Chicken soup. Thank you genius part of my brain. Perfect. I bought bouillon cubes and a special chicken and garlic seasoning. You have got to start somewhere. A Chicken Soup Candle was my somewhere. Oh, Oprah, you are so going to love these!

It was after midnight when I started to melt my non·scented candles into a Dutch oven on top of my stove. Go ahead, just call me the Pioneering Revolutionary Woman of the West. I was feeling organic. I was feeling 'pioneer·y'. I would have fit right in with the characters on Little House on the Prairie (google this show if you don't know what it is). Wait, that's a different era than the Revolutionary War. But you get my idea. I was transported back to a simpler time. When women honed their candle making skills. I was a vision of the past living in the 21st century.

I melted my wax. I sprayed PAM into the glass jar (the poor pioneer women didn't have the advantage of having PAM available back then. They probably used pig lard.) I added my special seasonings to the wax. Trust me, you could have pulled out a spoon and started slurping away. That candle wax was the sipping image (instead of spitting image...sipping image...my attempt at being punny...) of a bowl of homemade chicken noodle!

It was getting late. I was getting very sleepy. I poured the scented wax in the glass jar, attached the measured string around the pencil, and carefully laid the pencil across the rim of the jar. Mrs. Papp would have been proud. I would have received an A for that project.

I cleaned up a bit, and left the rest for the morning. I was the last one still awake. Everyone was already deep into their REM sleep cycle. I brushed my teeth and turned out the lights. It had been a full day. Tomorrow I would unveil my million dollar money maker. This was my last night to sleep as a middle class citizen. I'll need to invest in higher thread count sheets in a few weeks...

Morning came. My husband woke up. "What's that SMELL???" were the first words out of his mouth? I sniffed. I smelled it, too. "That's my Chicken Noodle Soup Meal Candle. I made it last night while you were sleeping!"

My enthusiasm didn't last long. I took my husband by the hand and led him downstairs to view my creation. Every step of descent brought the now slightly pungent odor more alive. The couches, curtains, and every porous material in the house had grasped hold of the waxy chicken and garlic scent. It wasn't good, my friends. It's not a scent you want in your house first thing in the morning, it's probably not a scent you would ever want in your home for that matter.

I so wanted to burn the candle. Yet I so wanted to keep my marriage intact. There's a reason candle companies sell candles with the scents of pumpkin, apple, and cinnamon. They are pleasing scents. They smell good anytime of the day. My attempt at recreating chicken soup into a wax product was a complete failure. Just like Dr. Frankenstein realized when his monster killed that little girl. Some things just aren't meant to be created. Some creations are better left in an uncreated state.

Oprah wouldn't be calling me. I would still have to be paying a mortgage and car payment, and my sheet thread counts would remain in the low hundreds. It was a good idea. If I just had a chemist who was a friend, and would be willing to work up a chemical equivalent of a turkey dinner without the ingredients of bouillon cubes, my idea STILL MAY WORK!

I'm not giving up. Perhaps one day you will walk into your local card and gift store, and think, "Hmmm, who's cooking homemade BBQ?" only to realize it is my CANDLE sitting on the table in front of you! A girl can still dream, can't she?

True, not every road to success is easy. You may end up having to walk barefoot in snow for miles uphill for years, but somewhere along the road, it has to take a turn. Spring comes, the snow melts, you find a pair of shoes, the road gets paved, and it starts to gently slope downward. We, at this time in our world have every opportunity to succeed in front of us. The world truly is your oyster. As Walt Disney stated, 'If you can dream it, you can do it'.

Don't give up on your dreams. Don't think all you will ever be able to do in life is just work a job, and never actually have a career doing something you love. Why those years of me selling weird bathroom accessories? Perhaps, because as a speaker and author, I am self-employed. My 'product'? *Me.* It may sound odd, but in order to get speaking engagements, I have to '*sell* me'. And those years of door-to-door sales gave me the confidence to sell! (Thanks, Mom and Dad)

Why all this talk about my past 'selling' career and failed meal candle idea? Because *every* bit of your past (even if you're only thirteen years old) will be used in your future. It's all shaping you into who you will be. Not a day is wasted (although there are a

lot of mundane boring days we live through).
Having your life matter in this world is a
combination of boring days, days when you
are learning about things you *can* do, and
experiences that will enrich your future.

Will your life be just a job? What do you
want to do with your future? Can you see
your present place in life as a tool that God is
using to bring you into a new place? Or does
your day-to-day make you feel as if you are
literally walking to and from 'school' uphill
both ways. Uphill *both* ways? Come on, that
just doesn't even make sense!

WHATCHYA WANNA BE?

I took a poll of my (old) friends yesterday. 'Guys and Girls that grew up in the 1970's, what did you want to be when you grew up?' was the question I asked. These friends of mine are an interesting bunch (and yes, old). I received quite the variety of answers.

GIRLS:
Airline Stewardess, Wonder Woman, Teacher, Mom, a Grocery Clerk at Piggly Wiggly, Nurse, Singer, Dental Hygienist, Married to a Preacher, Nurse in Africa, A Missionary to Africa (which is interesting, because that's usually what people fear God will call them to once they've become a Christian!), Cosmetologist, Secretary, and Fashion Designer were just a few of the

answers.

GUYS:
Professional Baseball Player, Batman, Preacher, Singer, owner of a Music Store, Fireman, and Funeral Director (although I have a funny feeling someone listed that last one as a joke).

Obviously, I had more women respond to my question. I don't have run-of-the-mill acquaintances. I'm sure the average elementary school student in the 1970's didn't wanted to be a preacher, but these are my friends. You should meet them someday. They keep me entertained.

I recall my own days in the early elementary grades. While the majority of my little female friends either wanted to be nurses or ballerinas, I most likely fell into the third most popular future career for little girls, and in particular little girls who loved animals. My future career would find me a veterinarian. I did indeed love animals of all shapes, sizes, and fluffiness levels.

My goal in being a full-time veterinarian was to be able to earn enough money to buy a huge farm, and go rescue all of the stray cats and dogs of every humane society, and bring them to live forever in peace, harmony, and safety on my farm. The End.

Well, that dream did in fact end. It ended with the stark realization that in order to be a veterinarian, I would have to administer shots to animals. Even if they were to make them healthy, I couldn't see myself giving shots, because I, myself, hated them. How could I have a career doing something I hated, even though I would be able to work with animals every day? That dream died, but new ones inevitably took its place.

Boys, on the other hand had some very grand aspirations for their futures. Cowboys, astronauts, the President of the United States, Batman and other Superheroes were common goals of many little boys. Not many children said that when they grew up, they just wanted to make ends meet and bring in a paycheck large enough to cover that month's bills and expenses. No, they dreamed big, and spoke from their hearts.

I believe who we are created to be, and our personal career calling, is placed within us from the time we are inside of our mother's womb. God looks at each individual embryo, and pours specific giftings and talents into each of us. No two are given the same ingredients for identical gifts.

Ephesians 2:10 says, 'For we are God's workmanship, created in Christ Jesus to do good works, which God prepared in advance for us to do.' God already prepared you for a specific vocation. I love the definition for the word vocation: A strong feeling of suitability for a particular career or occupation. Where do you find that 'strong feeling of suitability'? I believe it's already deep within you, placed there by the Creator himself.

I came across a portion of scripture that leapt out at me concerning who we are and the gifts and abilities we have within us. It's a classic case of 'I've read that Bible verse a gazillion times, and it never meant anything to me until that one time'.

The passage is found in Exodus 35: 30-35. "Then Moses said to the Israelites, "See, the LORD has chosen Bezalel son of Uri, the son of Hur, of the tribe of Judah, and he has filled him with the Spirit of God, with wisdom, with understanding, with knowledge and with all kinds of skills— to make artistic designs for work in gold, silver and bronze, to cut and set stones, to work in wood and to engage in all kinds of artistic crafts. And he has given both him and Oholiab son of Ahisamak, of the tribe of Dan, the ability to teach others. He has filled them with skill to do all kinds of work as engravers, designers, embroiderers in blue, purple and scarlet yarn and fine linen, and weavers—all of them skilled workers and designers."

Now, when I was attending Christian

college, and had to read the entire Old Testament as part of my Introduction to the Old Testament class, I fell asleep reading many of these types of passages. B-O-R-I-N-G. Boring until you discover that what you're reading can relate to your life. Now you may have to dig a bit to see why I included this verse, but I think it's a gem!

First off, I love Moses. He's my favorite person in the Bible. (Other than Jesus, of course. He's a given.) I love the relationship that Moses had with God. He could be honest and open with his creator. I think God really liked Moses' candid nature. Moses didn't hold back his feelings with God, and God could handle it. Perhaps I need to write a book about all the qualities I love about Moses.

So God was giving Moses all kinds of inside scoop on what he wanted and needed. Moses was his #1 go-to man to get things done. It was time to create the Ark of the Covenant, and I would be putting it mild to say that God was being specific in what he wanted. This God of ours is a detailed creator! God himself tells Moses who he wants to craft the Ark's details. There's just something that I love when God calls out Bezalel.

He knows him. God knows him *well*. 'Bezalel, son of Uri, son of Hur, tribe of

Judah'. God specifies his ancestry, as well as his address. I'm sorry, that just makes me smile. God knows your specifics. He knows everything about you and I. "You know Kirsten, daughter of Greg, birth daughter of Gary, at 9208 Branson Landing Blvd." I admire his detailed descriptions!

Moses tells the 'congregation' that God filled Bezalel with the Spirit of God (which is interesting, because the Holy Spirit hadn't been dispersed to humans yet...only in individual cases), and filled him with 'skill, ability, and know-how for making all sorts of things'. Then God goes on to describe in detail the skills Bezalel has, and ends with the fact that he is also gifted in every kind of skilled craft, including teaching!

God then lists some more very specific things that Bezalel and his friend, Oholiab (such different names back then) are gifted in. Really specific details!

Don't let these verses fly by. They're so good! God knows your ancestry, your address, *and* every tiny detail of talent he has put into you! He knows his creations by name! He hasn't forgotten what he placed inside of you from the very beginning of your creation.

What you're good at? God put that in you! What you love to do, and have discovered you can do well? He gave you those abilities.

You're not just some random creation. You are designed for a purpose. Our job is to live our lives using up every last drop of ability.

On a Saturday afternoon this past summer, while it was boiling outside, I enjoyed an afternoon of watching some of Oprah's last shows (you guys know who Oprah is, right?). She had a show where she showed clips from some of her favorite guests. One of her absolute favorites, was a little boy named Mattie Stepanek. Mattie appeared on the Oprah show many times over her last decade. He wrote many New York Times best-selling books, gave speeches across the country, and raised millions for MDA.

Watching the show, I heard a sentence that Mattie spoke to his mother as he was in his last days of life. "Have I done enough?" He was thirteen years old when he died. He had influenced Presidents and people across the world, yet he wanted to know if he had 'done enough' in his short life. Had he fulfilled everything he was meant to do while alive on this planet.

How many of us ask that of ourselves? Have I done enough? Have I done enough with what God has given me? You may be the age that Mattie was when he passed on. You may be older. Knowing that God is the giver of your talents, are you doing enough with what he's placed inside of you? Have I done enough? I ask myself the same question. A question worth asking ourselves year after year.

Somewhere between the elementary school playground and the time we take our first job out of college, the ballerina shoes are set in a storage box, and the astronaut helmet is sold at a garage sale. The hopes and dreams we had in our innocent years are replaced with the more grounded realization that you should be grateful to even find a place that would hire you. Life isn't so much about what you would love to *be* someday, it's more about making a paycheck and paying bills. Dreams are for the young. This is real life.

In middle school, I went with my parents to see a married couple give a concert at a church in town. Their names were Denny and DeAnza Duron. Denny was a semi well-known football player. He and his wife were just gorgeous. They sang together. As I watched them sing together on stage, a new dream was born. I had a new vision of what I want to be when I 'grew up'. I wanted to be the Durons! I wanted to travel and sing with a handsome husband, just like DeAnza. Forget Veterinary School. I wanted to sing and travel! Well, I also wanted to be in commercials, but I was pretty sure I would be able to combine both those careers quite smoothly.

That dream continued. After I graduated from college, I toured with a USO sponsored group called Re-Creation.

Our group performed shows in Veterans Administration hospitals across the country (the men and women who have served in the armed forces). We would personally visit all of the patients, and then literally wheel most of them down to see the show. When we weren't at a VA, we were busy doing convention shows to raise support for the VA work we did. We also had a church program. We were busy. We traveled the country. I loved it.

The only thing missing was that gorgeous singing husband. I always assumed that I would get engaged during the last year of college, and journey into my newly graduated life a married woman. I thought an MRS degree went hand-in-hand with a BS degree. As I found out, good things really do come to those that wait.

After a year with the USO group, my parents told me about a singing group that had an opening for a female singer. That group was called Eternity.

I had been with Re-Creation a whole year, when the group Eternity was nearby in concert. We actually had a day off, so I went to both hear their concert as well as audition for them. I hate auditioning. Is that awful? You are nervous, and never do as well as 'normal' because you are being judged for that one song you sing. Not my comfort zone!

My good friend from Re-Creation went with me. While we were parking the car, I saw this version of my ultimate Dream Man step outside of Eternity's bus, and get his luggage out of the bus bins. He took my breath away. You know how you have this image of exactly what you want your spouse to look like? Well, he was it. Down to every last detail.

We got out of the car, and at this point, there were hundreds of butterflies in my stomach. Butterflies for this impending vocal audition, as well as my anticipation for meeting this Dream Man of mine. I walked up to the bus and introduced myself to him. B-I-N-G-O. This man was the vocal director for the group. The head honcho. The man in charge. I liked that. I liked him immediately. He even dressed really well. Stop the presses, I had found my ideal man.

He led my friend and I into the place where the rest of the group was having dinner. After introducing me to everyone, he excused himself. He was going upstairs to take a shower and get ready for the concert. I immediately missed him as he vanished behind the railing. What was happening with me?

The concert was great. I couldn't keep my eyes off this vocal director. He was 'Denny'. He was what I imagined my Denny Duran to be. I could be his DeAnza. My middle school dream of singing and touring with my future husband was fleshing itself out before my very eyes.

This vocal director had me sing Amazing Grace. It was the 1980's. That's just the song everyone used for any kind of audition. "I would like to ask you a few questions", this vocal director asked during my audition time. I was prepared to say "Yes. Yes, I will marry you if you ask me right now. Now about the ring..."

He asked me questions of what I had done vocally over the years, and then I got bold, and thought to ask him a few questions myself. "Where do you see *yourself* in five years" came out of my mouth.

"Well, I'd love to be married. My dream has always been to have a bus or motor home, and travel doing concerts with my wife and family."

What? Could this be? This has always been MY dream! Well, only my dream after the whole veterinarian dream died. Look at this man. He is physically everything I adore, and now we share the same dream?

When he told me his potential future life scenario, I thought to myself, *'Don't you dare tell him that is your dream, too. That would scare him away faster than speeding bullet. Be wise...'*

I restrained myself from telling him all about Denny and DeAnza Duron, and the fact that if he married me, he would be helping to fulfill a dream that I had since 6th grade. Look who's getting all grow'd up! Such a big girl now!

Well, my friends, I met Dave Hart twenty-seven years ago as he interviewed me for Eternity's singing position, and we have enjoyed twenty-six years of the most romantic-filled, singing-filled, traveling-filled, motor home living-filled, child-raising filled years a girl could dream for. And for that ring? Heart-shaped and beautiful! Heart/Hart. Cute, huh!

Trust me, singing and touring with my hubby has been way more fulfilling than neutering and spaying cats and dogs would have ever been! God placed within me a dream that would 'use up' the giftings that he poured into my embryonic DNA. He made me who I am, in order that I would fulfill my calling and purpose for living.

Who have you always wanted to be? What are you always dreaming of doing with your life? Perhaps if your dreams aren't being fulfilled, you can take those ballerina slippers out of the attic and try them on again. Stick an astronaut helmet on your head. Remember that feeling of adventure? That thrill of 'what could be'? It's all out there for you. All of those dreams are still inside of you. It's time to start bringing them alive.

AIN'T NUTHIN' YOU CAN DO

Perhaps you think you don't have any talent. You aren't singing before thousands of people, or on TV, or in the movies, or flying to space, or changing the political system, or creating Meal Candles (sorry...just had to throw that one in the mix). Your name hasn't been in lights, and no one really notices you. You blend in. You're insignificant in the world's eyes. You're nothing special. You just roam the halls at school. You sit by yourself at lunch.

Well, (cue fanfare music) I'm here to tell you differently. (Play fanfare music) You are a Child of the King! You are significant! You are important! You *do* make a difference in this world! You matter! You were born for greatness.

Now, don't get me wrong here. I'm not

implying that if you work a 9-5 job making minimum wage, that you aren't important. Not everyone is created to be in the movies, or on TV. The world is full of people influencing the world and using every ounce of their giftedness in what some people would call mundane careers. It's all in the attitude. It's all in your approach to life. It's all in how you see your life making a difference in this world.

So we have this guy at our local Taco Bell. There's only one Taco Bell in the town we are living in right now. The Harts are Taco Bell connoisseurs. I'll never forget the first time our oldest son, Tyler, ordered his very first "meximelt with no pico sauce, please" on his very own. We gave him a dollar and some change, and he could barely see over the metal counter (he's not extraordinarily short, it was just when he was much younger). It was dear and near to my heart. My baby, ordering his own meximelt. Some moments stay in your heart forever. Ah...sweet Taco Bell.

Getting back to this guy at our local Taco Bell. Last summer was our first summer here. We had just moved every last belonging to this new town of ours. What was our dinner of choice? You guessed it, 'the Bell'. We were using the drive-thru, and the voice from the 'ORDER HERE' box surprised us.

That was an interesting woman's voice, we all thought. We pulled around to the 'PAY HERE' window, and a man was standing there. That was odd. Perhaps a separate woman takes the orders, and this is just the cashier guy. When I was handing this window guy my debit card, I learned that my assumption was wrong. This indeed was the same voice that took my order. Hmm, what an interesting voice!

As life would have it, we continued to frequent this Taco Bell establishment. We were always greeted by the same voice. Now, to be honest, yes, we had a few giggles over the odd matching of the voice with the body. But here's the deal: we were *always* greeted with the most positive, upbeat greetings whenever we pulled next to the 'ORDER HERE' box. The 'Welcome to Taco Bell' was enthusiastic. There was excitement behind the taking of every order. I enjoyed giving this man my order. It made me smile.

It took me a few weeks to realize that this employee was what schools term 'special'. But he was my favorite employee there. He had a job, and performed his role at 100% all the time! I loved him for it! I enjoy going to Taco Bell because of his excellent service. He is an example to those who work at fast food establishments. If everyone fulfilled their job roles to the extent that our Taco Bell man does, it could change the whole industry.

A few weeks ago, we went through the line, but another voice greeted us. *What?* Our guy wasn't working that day??? It just didn't seem right to order from someone else. Our Taco Bell run didn't seem complete. It felt wrong.

We were talking about this guy with our son Ryan's girlfriend, and she said that people post about our Taco Bell guy on a website about our town! I guess we're not the only family that thinks he's a fantastic employee! I love it. A 'No Talent Tom' he isn't! Hey, he made it into this book! He indeed did have a talent. He was exceptional in customer service. He made us happy to go to Taco Bell.

"But, Kirsten, you don't understand, I really don't have anything that I'm good at."

OK, if you feel that way, we need to work through a few things first. Come, lay down on this couch here. There ya go. That's right. Relax. Do you need a sip of water? That's good. Close your eyes. Now let's go back to your childhood.

The people I meet that feel as if they don't have any talent, or that there isn't anything special about them, grew up in environments where they were told that exact thing. Perhaps you've heard some of these following lines as you've been growing up:

You're too fat.
You're too skinny.
You're too tall.
You're too short.
You're not smart enough.
You're not pretty enough.
You're not handsome enough.
You can't.
You won't
No one in your family ever has, and neither will you.
Just deal with it.
You're not talented.
Where'd you come from?
We never wanted you in the first place.
You're nothing but a loser.
You're good for nothing'.
Don't expect anything out of life.
People like us don't become rich and famous.
You'll never amount to much.
You'll never make it out of this town.
Your dad/mom was a loser, and you'll be one too.

I could go on and on, but it's hard even writing those words. Do you feel like you were the only one who heard words like that? Don't. People across the world have had those ugly words directed at them thousands of years. If you fall into that category, you are in the company of greatness. Even though those words for the most part are painful to hear, and affect the psyche down deep, you can rise above them. You can prove them wrong. Albert Einstein did! And if he can do it, you can, too!

At the age of ten, Albert Einstein began attending the school at Luitpold Gymnasium (a school not a gym). Although he was bright in school, his Greek teacher spoke the words, "You will never amount to anything" to him. Could you imagine? I hope that horrible teacher lived enough years to see who Albert turned out to be. Talk about needing to take words back!

After 'high school' (he was in Europe, so the schooling years were a bit different from our typical high school years here in the States), he applied to Zurich Polytech in Switzerland. How did he do? He FAILED his entrance exam!

Without Albert Einstein, we would never have known the theory of relativity (which, quite honestly I still don't really understand), Quantum mechanics (there's a reason why I'm a speaker and not a scientist), the Photoelectric Effect, The Brownian Movement, the Atomic Theory of Matter, and most importantly, WHY THE SKY IS BLUE.

Some of you science junkies will

understand everything that I just wrote. To me, it's all very confusing.

The point of all of this? Albert Einstein was one of the greatest minds to have ever walked on the planet earth. Pure genius. Yet, if he had believed what his Greek teacher said about him, he would never have come into his purpose for being alive. That purpose? To confuse so many high school students who have to study and memorize his theories in Physics classes! (Just kidding, you smarty-pants science brainiacs.)

I'm starting to feel out of my comfort zone. Science classes weren't my forte in school. I liked English better. Recess was the best. I have now regressed to my elementary school brain. OK, if I'm going there, Art was actually my favorite class. In particular when we were able to play with papier-mâché. The polar opposite of quantum physics.

Albert Einstein wasn't the only famous person to rise above what people told them. Abraham Lincoln, our sixteenth President of the United States, grew up exceptionally poor.

Abraham was born in a tiny log cabin with no window or a floor. His father could not read and hated to work. Abraham only had one year of schooling. His mother died when he was eight years old. His father remarried, and his new stepmother was the one responsible for teaching Abraham how to read. Reading was the key. It opened up a whole new world of possibilities for him.

Although he was strong and very personable, Abraham didn't come from the background you would expect for President of the United States of America. Even though he was uneducated and poor, he rose above his circumstances, and became one of the most well-known and respected presidents we have ever had.

Never think that your previous or present circumstances determine who you will become. God can use even those who have been told they would amount to nothing. Don't believe the lies that if neither of your parents succeeded that you will follow in their same footsteps. You were created for greatness. You can become the first in your family to succeed. Perhaps you are the next President of the United States! Now don't laugh. You never know!

So now you're beginning to realize that you may actually have some talent! Welcome to this side of the fence! It's nice over here. This is the side where you realize that you do have talents and gifts. You can make a difference in this world. You can *matter*. You were created to do something extraordinary with your life.

Pull up a chair and sit for a spell. Sweet Tea? Lemonade? Chocolate-chip cookies? Come and sit with me on this new 'Porch of Potential'. We have both rocking chairs and Adirondack chairs available for your relaxing pleasure. Put your feet up. Get comfortable, you're going to like it here. Ahhh, isn't the breeze just delightful? Another cookie?

"But Kirsten, I really don't have any special talents." Dear, dear one. Yes you do! Perhaps you just haven't uncovered what you're so good at yet. "More sweet tea?" Let's chat for a while. Mama Kirsten will help you unveil who you were always destined to be. This is going to be fun.

First, let's get cleaned up. Let's wash our hands of all the negativity you've ever heard your whole life. Of course, words are hard to scrub away. It may take some time. We've got time. Now get a cool clean washcloth and wipe that sweat and dirt off your face.

There. See it now? See that beautiful/handsome face! God created that face, and I believe he actually smiled when he formed your nose, mouth, cheek bones, and beautiful expressive eyes. Why, look at them sparkling!

Now get back in your chair. Isn't it beautiful out today? Why I believe the old thermometer on the porch is reading 73°, which just happens to be my favorite temperature. Such a perfect non-humid feel with the sun shining warm. OK, Darling, let's find *you*.

.

SECRET INGREDIENT

I really do love cooking and baking. I have been quite the cookbook collector over the years. My favorites? The ones from churches. You know, when the old women of the church decide to combine all of the church's best recipes over the past 150 years into a spiral bound collections of favorites? They're chock full of seriously the best recipes you will ever find. Not necessarily the *healthiest* recipes...but good ones.

I had so many recipe books, that a few years ago during a move, I decided to narrow down my collection. Talk about a pain equivalent to pulling out your nails! To choose between my 'babies'? How could a loving mother do that? They were all my beloved children.

Of course, the church cookbooks made the 'keep' pile. My book on Authentic Chinese Cooking had never been used, although the thought that one day I would create authentic Chinese cuisine for my family of four was still intriguing. 'Sell' pile it went. Who am I kidding? I couldn't even pronounce the majority of ingredients in that book. Squid Soup? No thanks.

The save or sell process was excruciatingly long. Yes, no, *maybe*? The books with the simple ingredient dinners and desserts were all kept. They were more my style. The easier the better. The book full of dessert recipes that simply used a box of cake mix as the foundation for every recipe was so totally kept. I love that book. Have you ever made chocolate-chip cookies from a box cake mix? You'd love 'em. So easy and good. I'll send you the recipe. Impress your friends!

You want it now?

Just take a box of cake mix. ANY flavor you would like. Combine the cake mix with ½ cup of butter melted and 2 eggs. A little splash of vanilla for good measure? Sure! That is your cookie base. Next add any fun ingredients you wish, or just stick with plain perfection: chocolate-chips. Bake at 350° for 10 minutes. You will thank me later. Bring them to school, and I promise you will have more friends than you can handle.

I recently read an article written by Anne Beiler. She is the founder of Auntie Anne's Pretzels. If you have never devoured one of her famous pretzels, you are missing out on one of the best reasons to be grateful you are alive at this point and time in human history. They. Are. Delicious. I have had many for my lunch. That's right. Just a pretzel for lunch. I don't live with my mommy and daddy anymore. If I want to eat only a pretzel for lunch, I can. One of the perks of being a grown up.

In this article, Anne was telling the story of how her pretzel empire was born. She was raised in the Amish-Mennonite community of Lancaster, Pennsylvania. I remember going there as a child. I always loved the Shoo-Fly Pie. Oooh, and the homemade breads were out of this world.

In order to support her husband's vision of being a counselor, Anne bought a concession stand at a local farmer's market. They sold all kinds of foods, including fresh-rolled pretzels. All the other foods were selling well, except for the pretzels. She was contemplating removing the pretzels from their menu.

When talking with her husband about deleting the pretzels, he mentioned that an aunt of his had made delicious pretzels when he was growing up, and perhaps Anne could talk with his aunt about her pretzel recipe. They indeed tried the new recipe, and the pretzels have since become literally world famous!

Anne was close to actually taking the pretzels off the menu! Now, whenever you hear the words Auntie Anne's, all you think about are those buttery, perfectly baked bites of deliciousness. I want one right now.

She was just missing a few key secret ingredients. Just a few new ingredients changed the whole recipe, and made the difference! Her company is now worth millions and millions of dollars, is found in forty-four states, and over twenty-two countries! And to think she almost gave up on the pretzels!

You are my 'little pretzel'. If you are feeling like you are a product that should be 'taken off the menu' hang in there. We just need to discover your secret ingredients! It's that simple. By the way, if after reading this book, you happen to change your net worth to the millions category, I would like to request a 10% commission. I'm not kidding. 10% straight off the top. And the rights to your first movie. And your first child.

So. You want to discover what your special giftings are. What makes you stand out from the crowd. What sets you apart.

Your personal mission. What your secret-no-one-else-has-it ingredient is? This, you're going to enjoy. Hopefully. Of course, I'm one of those odd creatures that always enjoys doing the 'personality tests'. I suppose that is my personality category! 'Hello, I'm a melancholy', 'Hello, I'm a passive-aggressive'...."HELLO, My name is Kirsten, and I'm an Enjoying Personality Test Taker. Nice to meet you."

This won't hurt you one bit. I promise. No list of 1000 questions. I'll even be super nice. If you don't want to be involved in this activity, you can skip right over this whole section. You will hurt my feelings, and possibly not discover a hidden talent that could make you famous one day, but I want to give you that option. I'm setting you free. If you love someone, set them free. If they come back they're yours; if they don't they never were. (I think I wrote that quote in letters to a few boyfriends in the 1980's).

So I will begin by asking you a few simple questions. Do you have your #2 pencil sharpened and ready? You don't? That's OK, remember, I told you this would be pain-free. No pencils required for Mrs. Hart's class. I'm the cool teacher.

What do you love to do? It sounds so simple, doesn't it. Believe it or not, some people have never taken the time to sit down and ponder what they love to do. What you love to do usually helps define your skills and passion. Most of us wouldn't list things that we're bad at doing in our list of 'things we love to do'. Usually the things you love to do, you're naturally good at. I don't love to do math because I'm horrible at it. I love to sing. I love to bake. I love to decorate my house. These are activities that I love to doing, and that other people have confirmed 'you're pretty good at this'.

Ever feel like it's overly 'braggy' to talk about what you're good at? This is a new day! I am here to announce that it is not prideful to know your gifts and passions. It's not wrong to talk to others about what you're good at. Now if you start getting too big for your britches, and thinking that you're better than everybody else, we may need to sit and have a chat. You don't want to be *over* enthusiastic to your friends about what you're so good at. Nobody likes a bragger. But, you *do* need to learn and realize what God has put inside of you.

I've met some sweet, sweet people, and have asked them what they're good at. "Well, nothing, really…" is a response I have too often heard. So sad. People have gone their whole lives thinking there's nothing that they're particularly good at. Ask the same question, "What do you love to do?", and you get a whole different response.

My grandfather used to have a huge garden in his side yard in Erie, Pennsylvania. Not a fancy man, my Grandpa Caldwell. He was a welding specialist at a factory there, yet he also produced some of the best corn and tomatoes you could ever put inside your mouth. I'm sure if you were to ask him what he was good at, he would have replied, 'Oh, nothing in particular', yet he was one of the best garden farmers ever. I know he enjoyed working in his garden, but yet wouldn't particularly say that he was good at it. He could have easily sold his produce at farmers markets, and won blue ribbons. He indeed was good at what he loved doing.

I know I was joking earlier about needing a sharpened #2 pencil. Well, if you have the time, I would love for you to write down a list. You won't be graded on this, and you can use a pencil *or* a pen. Whatever your heart desires to write with.

Next, make a list. This list should include all the things you're good at. This list can be as simple or complex as you wish. Are you good at cleaning windows? Write it down. Are you good at photography? Write it down. If you're worried about someone else in your household seeing this list, and them getting the idea that you're becoming a Diva or

'Divo', then hide the list. They can make up their own list if they so choose to read this book. (Now who's talking like a Diva???)

I'll be nice and give you a few starting ideas. You may have similar interests to this list, or the things listed may be polar opposites of what you feel your gifts are. Either way, it's a good start to you creating your own list.

- Building things
- Fixing things
- Investigating things
- Making connections
- Building relationships
- Creating dialogue
- Healing wounds
- Adding humor
- Persuading people
- Organizing things
- Selling things
- Doing the numbers
- Resolving disputes
- Instructing others
- Optimizing things
- Making deals
- Starting things
- Designing things
- Researching things
- Seeing the big picture
- Writing things

- Solving problems

Get carried away. Have a blast. You're not being prideful, you're recognizing the gifts God has put into you. This is healthy, trust me. Much healthier than the candy corn I have been nibbling on while writing this chapter.

Now take that #2 pencil and sharpen it again. I know. I lied. I said you weren't going to have to use a pencil. Will you forgive me? Blame it on the nature of the beast. The beast of finding your inner gifts. But that would be a nice beast wouldn't it. Again, if you want to skip this exercise, feel free. But I think you may enjoy it.

Here's what I want you to do. Answer by writing the very first thing that comes to mind with the following questions. Don't take a lot of time thinking about each item. The quicker you answer, the more pure the answer. OK, here you go:

• As a young child, what did you love to do? Write? Read? Sports? Playing with Legos? Experimenting with a chemistry set? Spending time outdoors? Pretending to be a solider or a spy? Baking? Sewing?

• During school group projects, what job do other students assign to you, or do you volunteer for?

• What aspects of your current job (if you have a job) do you love? Which can't you stand?

• What kinds of projects and jobs at home and school do you get excited about? What kinds do you dread?

• Have you ever talked to a friend about a topic, a dream, or an aspiration and everything just clicked inside of you, and you felt a surge of excitement throughout your body?

• What issues get you really fired up?

• What things do you see other people doing that make you (in a good way?) envious because you wish you were doing them?

• What were you doing the last time you totally lost track of time?

Are all these questions overwhelming you a bit? I totally understand. Take a little break. Perhaps you need to go get yourself a glass of chocolate milk, or make yourself a s'more. Those two items usually comfort and relax me.

Are you done with your little break? Time to dig in just a little more. I promise the rest of the chapters will feel like a cake walk after this one!

Now, this may take some of you *way* out of your comfort zone, but trust me, it's all worth it. Live a little. Go a little farther out on the branch. Trust me for a bit, will you? The end result will be worth it all.

Here's what you can do. Brace yourself. Here we go. Ask some of your friends what they think you're good at. GASP! See, now, this would be as natural as breathing to me. Of course, I'd try to make it rather humorous, but this activity lines right up with my taking those Personality Tests. I wasn't a shy one in school. Can you tell?

Now get ready to be surprised. Unless they're all horrible to you and say that you're not good at anything. If that is the case you need to get new friends. I'll be your friend. Don't worry. I know I could find things you're good at!

Does it freak you out to ask someone what they think you are good at? Try not to think about it too long and hard. Friends sometimes can see things about us that we can't see ourselves. I'll bet you'll be shocked at what people will tell you. 'Me? You think I'm good at that?' I'm smiling right now thinking about how (hopefully great) this activity will work out for you.

So take your multiple paged list of what you're good at. Look at it long and hard. Give yourself a big smile. Give yourself a hug. You are so talented. God has given you so many giftings. See? Slap yourself on the back. 'Well look at me, I do have things I'm good at.' Now, you don't have to go around the house telling your whole family that you just found out you are indeed God's gift to the world. A little humility is a nice thing.

Congratulations. Now I want you to work on another list. Don't worry, I'm not requiring you to come up with all these lists in the same day. If you're an overachiever, go for it. If you struggled just to come up with a few items for the last list, take a breather. No pressure. Just somewhere down the road take out another piece of paper and jot down these thoughts.

What excites you?

That's your question. This time don't think long and hard. Just start freely writing what excites you in life. What do you love? What are you passionate about? What gets your heart racing?

What excites you could be a hobby, a side job, something you do as a volunteer. It could be something you haven't done in a long time. On your marks, get set, GO!

Are you exhausted? I know. This is a lot of

work. I think you'll enjoy the end result. You might even stir up some life passions that you didn't know you had. Self-discovery can be a great thing. It's energizing.

FINAL LIST details: (I hope this one is fun for you, too). Now write down what you have secretly dreamed of doing (even if it's a new dream). Have fun with this. This is your time to go crazy, my friends. Again, this is *your* list. Brainstorm. If you want to share this list with your family and loved ones, go for it. If not, keep it for yourself. Whatever floats your boat.

Have you wanted to be a novelist, an artist, a designer, an architect, a doctor, a professional athlete, an entrepreneur, or programmer? Maybe there are several careers or goals you have dreamed about. Add them to the list, no matter how unrealistic you may think they are.

Now take a Caribbean cruise and enjoy reading all of your lists. Go ahead. You'll enjoy it. You deserve it. Tell your parents I told you to go. I'll take the blame.

When you're back from the cruise, take your lists out again. Granted, you may have to wipe all the sand off the papers, but it'll be worth it.

Now re-glance over your lists. Do you see any common threads? Do you see any items that appear on all the lists? Is there something on the lists that has inspired you? Didn't realize that you were good at something that a friend saw in you? Could that untapped gift work in unison with that dream career you have always thought about? 'Gosh, Joe said that I was great at fixing computers. I never thought I was that good at it? Perhaps I could repair computers as I side job while I'm still in school'.

A whole new world of possibilities awaits you. Perhaps you have realized new dreams. God is the giver of dreams, and I promise you, he's not done creating, or giving dreams. Perhaps he's waiting to give you a brand new passion that will excite you beyond what you thought possible for your life.

The best, my friends, is still to come! If you haven't realized your secret ingredient yet, keep searching. It's bound to be somewhere in the cupboard of your heart. See it? Maybe you have to reach way in the back, but it'll be worth it. Once you add that secret ingredient to your life, there's no stopping you. Get ready to take off! Your mission is launching.

MR. & MRS. DOWNER

I don't want to take forever on this chapter. Although it is an important one. The purpose of writing this chapter? *Stay away from negative people.* I know you're thinking, 'Easier said than done'. Trust me, I understand.

I'm not old. Well, not really old. I am currently fifty years old. Granted to you, fifty might sound ancient. I get it. But I love my age. I am no longer referred to as 'such a child' and yet no one is signing me up for the local nursing home. This is a great age. I have lived enough life that people will fairly respect my opinion now, yet young enough to still enjoy platform shoes.

One thing I have learned in my fifty years

of living? The kinds of people I like to surround myself with. I like funny people. I like intelligent (but not too intelligent) people. You know what I mean. Some really smart people can only talk about things like Pythagorean theorems and the theory of relativity. My brain doesn't function in theorems. I function in the latest episodes of certain reality TV programs, and great new recipes I found online. Mine is a simpler existence.

I like people that share common interests. I like people that can step up and do what it takes in a situation, and not complain. I like encouraging people. I like positive people. I like people that make me laugh, and look on the bright side of life.

We recently had dinner with some friends in Orlando when we were down there. (You'll read about my Space Mountain experience later on in the book). I had met this couple before, but had never shared a meal together, or got beyond the 'nice to meet you's'. Dave knew them well, but it had been twenty-four years since he had been around them.

We met for dinner at 6:30. We closed the place down at 11, when the waiters started hauling out the vacuum cleaners. There hadn't been one single awkward pause. No "I think I may run to the restroom because this is completely boring me and I need a break" incident. We had non-stop wonderful stimulating conversation, and in fact continued chatting once we were standing outside of the restaurant.

That kind of scenario is *gold* to me. It doesn't happen all the time, and when it does, you know you have connected in a way with someone that is so precious and rare. Those are the friendships that I want to foster.

I don't want you to think that I will only associate with those who share similar interests. Believe you me, as a Worship Pastor's wife, I have learned that it is wise (and a blessing) to spend time with all kinds of people. And I have. But in all the years of meeting and greeting and eating, I have come to realize the kind of person that is stimulating and uplifting to be around. Those are the people I choose to be around when I have a choice.

Let's say you're a fireman (I realize you're a *student*, but go with me on this one). Now, you can go out to eat with all sorts of people, but when you have the opportunity to be with a group of other firemen, there is a common bond, and thread that ties you all together. Fellow firemen can relate to you in a way that computer graphic artists never could. You see what I'm saying here, yes?

But there's more. It's vital to who you are, and who God is turning you into, to be surrounded by positive people. Now I'm about to say something rather gutsy. Buckle up. It may be a rough ride. *You need to break off relationships with those that tear you down and discourage you.*

You still with me?

I know I said that I was going to make this chapter short, but whole volumes of books could be written on the topic of breaking off unhealthy relationships. Even high school friends! Can you think of someone right now who discourages you and tears down your thoughts and dreams? Have you continued in that relationship because you want to, or because you think it would hurt their feelings to walk away from them?

There are all kinds of reasons why we stay in unhealthy relationships and friendships. But I want to challenge you a bit right now. If you are surrounded by dream and vision stealers, you will never fully evolve into who you were designed and created to be. You will never be wholly *you* if you listen to all the negative voices.

The tough part? Some of these negatively voiced people are your own family members. You're stuck with them, right? Perhaps you can't decline the acceptance to the annual Thanksgiving Day festivities, but you can filter the time spent talking directly with them. You can filter how much time is spent in their presence. You can filter how many times you hear them on the phone cutting your ideas down. You can filter their ramblings. Have you heard of Caller I.D.? It's genius. Now I'm not promoting rudeness, but I am promoting self-preservation. And if your parents are calling...well, you kinda gotta pick up.

If God has called you to a certain purpose in life, and you continue to surround yourself with those who verbally cut you and your calling, you need to make a choice. Choose between God's plan for your life, or to be stuck in a rut with those pulling you down.

I know this is hard stuff. I know it's not easy. But I want you to live whole. Whole in your ultimate calling and purpose. Fulfilled, not frustrated. Inspired, not irritated.

If you feel that indeed there are some people that you need to start filtering out their involvement in your life, hold fast. First Peter 4:4-5 talks about what happens with old friends, once you have become a Christian, but I believe these verses also apply to letting go of unhealthy friendships. "Of course, your old friends don't understand why you don't join in with the old gang anymore. But you don't have to give an account to them. They're the ones who will be called on the carpet—and before God himself."

Jesus, himself understands letting go of those who do not believe the way you do. He had towns and villages full of people that rejected what he had to say. When Jesus first sent his disciples out on their own to 'drive out evil spirits and to heal every illness and sickness', he gave some specific instructions and great wisdom concerning the people they were to stay with.

"When you enter a town or village, look for someone who is willing to welcome you. Stay at that person's house until you leave. As you enter the home, greet those who live there. If that home welcomes you, give it your blessing of peace. If it does not, don't bless it. Some people may not welcome you or listen to your words. If they don't, shake the dust off your feet when you leave that home or town." Matthew 10: 11-14.

In Biblical times, when leaving Gentile cities, pious Jews often shook the dust from their feet to show their separation from Gentile practices. If the disciples shook the dust of a Jewish town from their feet, it would show their separation from Jews who rejected their Messiah. The gesture was to show the people that they were making a wrong choice. The opportunity to choose Christ might not present itself again.

Such great instruction. We need to take those words into our own lives, as we go about trying to make a difference in our world. If you're not accepted or welcome, shake the unwelcome dust off your feet, and move on. Move on to other relationships that are positive and welcoming. Move on to relationships that speak words of life, not discouragement.

You may not be able to jump head in on the whole distancing yourself from unhealthy relationships, but find a place to start. Start with baby steps if you need to. If every time you talk to a particular friend, you find yourself discouraged afterward, start limiting those calls. It's okay to monitor your calls. Trust me. There's no law that states you have to talk to everyone that calls you. Be selective. Be wise. Guard your heart and your dreams.

It's not easy. I know. Neither is losing weight, but I tell you, once you have dropped even ten pounds, you don't ever want to be walking around with that extra weight again. You never knew you could feel so good. It's the same with unhealthy relationships.

Another Bible verse: I John 2:19 is in reference to antichrists who tried to deceive people. I, personally feel it also refers to those who come against us, and try to harm us. "They left us, but they were never really with us. If they had been, they would have stuck it out with us, loyal to the end. In leaving, they showed their true colors, showed they never did belong."

There are people in the world who are dream and vision stealers. They want to suck the very life out of you. They're jealous. They want to discourage you. They feel bad about themselves, so in order to make themselves look and feel better, they drag you down to their level. Be strong. Resist. Rise above.

THE PRINCIPAL'S OFFICE

Now first off, I need to address something in the title of this chapter. I, like so many other wide-eyed innocents in elementary school learned how to spell principal with a cutesy little trick. Teachers taught their students to spell principal, as in the head dictator of their school, in such a way as to remember that the principal is your *pal*, versus the other spelling, principle (which is something you try to hold true to when in the presence of a princiPAL).

My rebel life started early. In Mrs. Jones' third grade class, my two best friends, Madzy Besselar and Julianne Mulusky, and I thought we would be artistic and creative, and drew wonderful designs all over our spelling books. Now mind you, these weren't the school-owned hardback books that had to survive generations of third grade students. These were the soft-back workbooks that would be ours to keep forever once the last school bell of the year had sounded.

We thought our books looked so much better decorated with hearts and stars. Mrs. Jones didn't. I usually liked her. Mrs. Jones was one of the younger, prettier teachers that year. On this day, however, she had turned into the Wicked Witch of the West (even though we were in East Coast New Jersey).

She, in not a nice manner, told the three of us that we were to take the biggest erasers we could find, and go out in the HALL and erase every bit of our artwork. "Erase it all, until the books look brand new again."

The *hall*???!!! That was the corridor of shame in elementary school! And wasn't it just our good fortune that some of the neighboring classes had to line up to make their way to the lunch room at the very time we were sitting and erasing. The finger pointing and snickering was enough to make us feel like the most wanted criminals in the Wild West. We were bad girls. We had done something shameful. There were fingers pointing at us.

What we were doing was being creative, thank you very much. I haven't been in touch with Madzy and Julianne since junior high, but I can betchya they're creative and artistic women! Mean Mrs. Jones. Wonder what she's up to?

Middle school was my time when I met with the principal on a regular basis. I honestly think she hated me. Really. I was attending a small Christian school at the time, Mercer Christian Academy, with Satan as the principal. (I didn't just write that did I?) I can't believe I forgot the name of the principal. Gosh, what was it? See, she was so mean that my self-conscious has purposefully blocked her name from my memory. Thank you self-conscious! You got my back!

I was friends with the principal's daughter, Debbie. That's funny, I can remember her daughter's first name, but not the last. AHHH! It just came to me! Mrs. MILLER! Do you know her? Not a nice woman.

So I was friends with her daughter, but we were in a *trio* with Dianne. There were the three of us: Dianne, Debbie, and Kirsten. Now, girls, you know what a threesome of middle school girls is don't you? TROUBLE with a capital T. Seriously. Perhaps four days out of the month, we were a happy trio of best friends. The other twenty-some days one of us was 'out'. Now raise your hand if you remember the whole 'out' thing. (Sorry guys reading this book, you'll just have to bear with me through this girl stuff. Take it as a freebie lesson in middle school female life.)

So, one friend may say something even a teeny weenie bit catty about one of the trio, and if we were in the mood, the one who said the comment would be 'out' until further notice. You were out of being 'in' the trio of friends. And, yes, periodically, even I was out sometimes. It's life in middle school. It's probably the basis for Darwin's Theory of Evolution. Survival of the fittest. (Well, actually Herbert Spencer originated that phrase, but Darwin used it later on). Needless to say, middle school was tough. Mrs. Miller was tougher.

It seemed as if every time that Debbie was 'out' I was 'in'. In the principal's office, that is. I think Debbie was telling to her mother. I also believe that Debbie got her revenge on the two who were keeping her 'out' by telling her mom things we did that would be possible reasons to visit the principal's office. Mrs. Miller was Debbie's personal mafia. 'You mess with my family, I mess with you...'

One of the times I was in Mrs. Miller's

office, I'll will admit, was justified. Mrs. Brown was my seventh grade teacher at Mercer Christian Academy. In fact, the school was so small that she was the only seventh grade teacher. On most days, she was nice. Not the coolest teacher in the world, but nice. One afternoon she was in a rather crotchety mood. Heck, I probably would have been, too, if I were stuck in a room with 7th graders day in and day out.

Well, I was not so thrilled to be sitting under the teacher-ship of Mrs. Brown that day. So, I thought it would be funny to randomly place a few thumbtacks on her desk chair. A few of the other students thought it would be funny, too, and dared and egged me on. I took the bait.

We had to wait until the math work on the board was complete, but then it happened. Mrs. Brown started walking towards her chair. When she pulled it out, I caught my breath. She sat down, and then immediately popped back up. I couldn't help it. It made me laugh.

"WHO DID THIS??!" she yelled. Every finger pointed in my direction. Busted. Back down to Mrs. Miller's office. Oh, joy.

Looking back now, I seriously can't believe I did that. Hey KIDS, don't listen to peer pressure! You'll end up in the principal's office, if not worse! Take this as a lesson from Mrs. Hart. Is it wrong to admit that the look on Mrs. Brown's face when she popped up was rather hilarious? It is wrong, isn't it.

The majority of the times that I got in trouble, I was getting in trouble for (hold your surprise here) TALKING TOO MUCH. Yeh, big shocker, huh. I, Kirsten Hart, talked too much. (I think I may have written something like that on the chalkboard a few times). But who's laughing now? I make a LIVING by talking! Lookie there! What I used to get in trouble for, is now how I make my living. I'm smiling as I'm writing this. "So there, Mrs. Miller."

Your talents, unrefined are usually what you got (or are getting) in trouble for in school. Refine those talents, and you'll find your great strength!

See, there's hope for all of us that visit the principal's office! We're just souls expressing our gifts that don't necessarily fit into the regimen and restrictions of a school building. We talkers were just communicators in need of the proper outlet. Once I discovered that I loved to speak before audiences, it's as if the 3rd grade girl in me came alive. No one told me to 'shush', and yet people actually listened to what I had to say!

I'm not alone. Know those class clowns that you laugh at in school? Lots of them might make the big bucks on stages before thousands, sharing their humor. Sent out to get on their CUSTOM COACH BUS instead of in the HALL!

You have seriously lived either under a rock, or in an Amish community if you have not heard of actor and comedian Jim Carrey (or you're too young to know his movies??). He has made umpteen movies, and is a bona fide Hollywood star. If probably wouldn't surprise you to find out that he was actually a class clown in school.

"Carrey has always been the class clown. His elementary school teacher, instead of punishing him for being rowdy and disruptive, made a deal. If Carrey would sit quietly during class without bugging his classmates, in exchange he would get a bit of time set aside at the end of every day to put on an act for them. It was in these early "performances" that he mastered his impressions and battled his self-proclaimed introversion and shyness." --An internet article written on Jim Carrey's life

See! Great, creative minds just need some guidance. I love that Jim's teacher gave him the reward of coming to the front of the class, and doing his impressions. I have read that during those post-class routines is where he created some of his well-known impressions that made him so famous. There's hope!

JustDisney.com shared an article about our beloved Walt Disney. "After Walt's birth, the Disney family moved to Marceline, Missouri. Walt lived out most of his childhood here. Walt had a very early interest in drawing, and art. When he was seven years old, he sold small sketches, and drawings to nearby neighbors. Instead of doing his school work Walt doodled pictures of animals, and nature.

His knack for creating enduring art forms took shape when he talked his sister, Ruth, into helping him paint the side of the family's house with tar."

No one would argue that Walt Disney wasn't one of the greatest creative minds and Imagineers of the twentieth century. Yet, even he 'doodled' instead of doing homework! Just think what I could have done with myself if Mrs. Jones hadn't stifled my creativity back in the 3rd grade!

Don't miss one of the best parts of Walt's childhood story. He and his sister painted the side of their HOUSE with TAR!!! I love it! Now there's a creative genius as a child. Am I giving some of you hope? Of course as children we need direction, but some of the greatest untapped talents and giftings appear in rather odd ways sometimes when we are young.

You know those boys that used to create

guns out of paperclips and endless rubber bands? Betchya they're engineers now! Those boys that used to non-stop build tinker toy bridges and fortresses? They've probably built skyscrapers!

What did you like to do as a young child that sometimes got you in trouble? Or (yikes) what are you *doing now* that you get in trouble for? Perhaps that was, or is your calling in an unrefined state.

There's always a silver lining. Sometimes you just have to search for it. Isn't God good? He can take what are seemingly our downfalls character-wise, and reinvent them into our strengths!

Now if you happen to paint tar all over your house to prove that you're the next Walt Disney, don't you blame it on me! I'll tell your parents it was *completely* your fault.

DUES

There are a few miracle stories of instant fame and recognition in this world. A Few. Most people just keep plugging away. Is this all to my life? No way. I still have gobs more I want to accomplish speaking-wise. My personal 'vision board' in my office is chock full. I plan on writing and speaking till the day I journey out of this world. I still have so much more to learn!

Have you heard the saying, "I've paid my dues", or "You have to pay your dues". Well, that really is part of life. 'Dues' are your stepping stones. Dues are where you learn.

I have paid some dues. I enjoy where I am in life right now, but I've had years of 'dues'.

When I toured with the group, Re-

Creation, I had a very prominent and important position. Yup, that's right, I was the monitor girl! Sounds important, doesn't it? Well, what my job actually consisted of was checking the placement of the monitors and speakers, and most importantly, running the sound cords. That's right. My responsibility was to make sure that the monitor and speaker cords were run correctly, and especially that they were taped properly. My best friend that year was gray duct tape. And yes, it is duct, not duck. So many call it DUCK tape. Novices.

I not only made sure the cords were run and taped in a perfectly aligned fashion, I also had to un-tape the cords after the show, and wrap up all of those sound cords in a neat and orderly manner. I took pride in my side job. I sang and was a 'show girl', and after the 'glamour' of singing, I was back to cord rolling. Paying my dues. There are advantages. I know some 'techie' stuff now. Hiring me to speak for a retreat, but need some sound cords run? I'm your girl. Trust me, those cords will look fabulous.

The year before I married Dave, I toured in Larnelle Harris' back-up group, Friends (Larnelle has won Dove awards (Christian music awards) and even Grammy awards!). Our first big tour with Larnelle was a Christmas Tour. We had sets, and stage decorations. Yes, I was a singer, and enjoyed singing every night with Larnelle, but my side gig? Setting up and tearing down that delightful set. Every night. We had white lighted snowmen placed across the whole stage. The snowmen were lit with dozens of little white light bulbs. Those light bulbs had to be screwed in every snowman before the concert, and screwed out afterwards, then placed back in special boxes every night. Every concert. *Dues.*

I do want to give a shout out to Larnelle Harris. Larnelle had proven himself, and paid his dues years before. Yet, he would help us disassemble the set decorations many nights. He would autograph every last record (I'm dating myself) or photo, then come on stage and see if we still needed any help. He's a great man. He never got 'too big for his britches'. I love that about him.

Paying your dues is the opposite of entitlement. You realize that there are steps to becoming the vision of your dreams. I didn't look at rolling monitor cords or tearing down Christmas sets as a job that was 'lesser' than what I deserved. It's all a process. I know behind the scenes information, now. I could fill in for some techie jobs, if I had to. I was gaining wisdom along the way. It's part of the process.

So what do you do in-between the

inception of a dream, vision, or goal, and its fruition? What did I do since starting to speak in the 1990's, and now? A lot. I worked at doing all I could to be a better speaker and kept pursuing better booking avenues. I looked at every speaking opportunity as a way to improve my skills. I 'paid my dues' by accepting every speaking event that came my way. Instead of thinking, "That isn't enough money", I accepted, and was grateful for the open door. And I didn't give up on my dream.

Yes, we all have a mission to fulfill while on this earth. But there are many different paths to that fulfilment. Some of those paths take years to walk. But know that God has his hand on you through every single year of paying your dues. Not a day is wasted.

On October 29th, 1941, the United Kingdom's Prime Minister, Winston Churchill, was asked to speak to the students of the Harrow School, where he had attended when he was a child. He gave the famous very short speech that people have quoted ever since. His words are my words to you today, "Never, ever, ever, ever, ever, ever, ever, give up. Never give up. Never give up. Never give up." Thank you, Mr. Churchill.

After struggling to develop a viable electric light-bulb for months and months,

Thomas Edison was interviewed by a young reporter who boldly asked Mr. Edison if he felt like a failure and if he thought he should just give up by now. Perplexed, Edison replied, "Young man, why would I feel like a failure? And why would I ever give up? I now know definitively over 9,000 ways that an electric light bulb will not work. Success is almost in my grasp." And shortly after that, and over 10,000 attempts, Edison invented the light bulb.

Never give up.

Never giving up is step one. It's simple. Stick with your dream. Don't forget your mission here sometimes takes years of processing. Accept every step along the way as an opportunity to learn more. Work on your craft. Perfect it. Keep creating. Keep visualizing. Keep planning. Never give up.

"It's all about who you know" is another keeper of a saying. I hate to admit it, but it really can be about who you know. It's also an important realization in the fleshing out of your God-given dream career and life goals. There are innumerable people who have great ideas. But if you know people who can take your invention, and get it in the hands of the right people, you are 'giant steps' ahead of everyone else.

Social media is a fantastic networking tool. A networking tool, but also a wonderful medium to stay in touch with people. I've been able to connect with people on social networking sites, that I would never have been able to contact on my own. Again, it's a case of 'I know this person, and they know that person, so therefore, I am able to get in touch with that person because of this person' (six degrees of separation). Now if you understood that, raise your hand. Anyone?

Stay connected. Find creative ways to be connected with the people that are influential in the field that you want to be in. Do you want to write books? Get in touch with those that are published, and are actively writing. Do you want to form your own band some day? Contact those bands, and get on their fan pages. Find out about their lives. Find out how they got where they are today.

Now I'm not promoting stalking! Although at rare times, I may be slightly guilty of mild stalking. Social media allows for some of that, thank you very much.

Do you have an invention that you're wanting to get recognized? Research who's out there inventing, and find out all you can about them. Stay connected, and get connected with the movers and shakers in the field that you're interested in. Those are the people that (when you have been able to prove yourself) can open doors for you that you could never open yourself!

Now, the third point of my three point sermon. Well, this isn't really a sermon, but I wanted to sound dignified. In seminary they teach pastors to have three points to their sermons, and I just happened to be bringing you a third point to waiting out your dream.

What to do while you're still in school, under your parent's authority, and not really on your own yet?? Let's review. Never give up and get to know more people in your 'dream field', because a lot of making your dreams come true is who you know. Now to the third and final point.

#3 Never burn your bridges.

Now if you have a literal bridge that you own, this is a given. Especially if you have one of those old New England-type beautiful red and white picturesque bridges. Do you own one of those? Never burn it. Please.

Okay, seriously. Don't burn your bridges=don't dismiss relationships. Don't walk away from a relationship in your life in a mean-spirited fashion. Now please understand me, if you have been in an abusive relationship, that is a totally different situation from what I am referring to right now. Abusive, bad, unsafe, unhealthy relationships? YES, walk away from those and don't go back.

In reference to not burning bridges, I am talking about people that have been or are presently in your life. Say, for example, for whatever reason, you leave a job (even if it's just a part-time job at McDonalds or Dairy Queen). That boss, and all the people you worked with are people that you need to keep an open relationship with. Do you need to picnic every weekend together? No. I am advising, whatever the circumstances for leaving the job, that you do your best to keep the relationship lines open. Don't bad mouth that boss on your way out. Don't make comments like, "Well, GOODBYE! You were the worst boss EVER!" and slam the door.

You know what will happen? That next position that you interview for will ask about your previous job. They'll want the name and previous phone number of your previous boss as a reference. Oh, and they'll call him/her, too. If you were ugly on your way out, that's the image that your boss will retain. That's the reference that your new possible boss will hear.

Don't burn the bridge.

We have to put forth the effort, and sometimes it takes a lot of effort to leave places and jobs with dignity and character without being spiteful and ugly. Burning a bridge is easy. A little gasoline and a match will do the job. Ka-Boom. It's gone. Maintaining a bridge takes a lot of work. You must keep up with repairs, and repaint when needed. If the wood is rotting, it must be replaced or fixed. Work? Yes, but worth it in the long run.

Never giving up, keeping and making connections with people, and not burning your bridges are ingredients for developing yourself into who you want to be, and for seeing your dreams materialize. Slow process? Sometimes. Worth seeing your dream come alive? Yep.

What does this chapter have to do with you at your age? "Um, Mrs. Hart, I'm just a high school student." I totally get that. But because I really like you, I want to give you a 'heads up' for the real world! I want you to *matter* and make a difference in this world. If something I have walked through as an adult, can help you through the next years of your life, then I will have a 'full circle moment'. What I walked through might help you→you learn by my example→you can help someone learn all of this by *your* example/story down the road.

#Circleoflife
#Watchthelionkingmovie
#thankmelater

APPLE SLICE

Steve Jobs, the co-founder of Apple, and revolutionary visionary just recently passed away. He is a prime example of following your heart and your dreams. Even though he dropped out of college, he had the dream to make computers available in homes. A dream that at the time was unheard of. One of my favorite Steve Jobs' quotes is this:

"Your time is limited, so don't waste it living someone else's life. Don't be trapped by dogma — which is living with the results of other people's thinking. Don't let the noise of others' opinions drown out your own inner voice. And most important, have the courage to follow your heart and intuition. They

somehow already know what you truly want to become. "

Believe for yourself that the best years are still to come. If you are given the chance, live out your dreams. You only pass through this life once. You are given one chance to be who you were created to be. Don't walk through life unfulfilled, or doing what someone *else* thinks you should do. Be wise, but live your life full. Be an inspiration to those around you. Inspire others to walk in their callings.

Being a leader in your home and school means leading by example. If you are living your life fulfilled, most likely your future children will, too. Your future spouse will be happier because you are happier, and you will enjoy life to its fullest.

"When I was 17, I read a quote that went something like: "If you live each day as if it was your last, someday you'll most certainly be right." It made an impression on me, and since then, for the past 33 years, I have looked in the mirror every morning and asked myself: "If today were the last day of my life, would I want to do what I am about to do today?" And whenever the answer has

been "No" for too many days in a row, I know I need to change something."

--Steve Jobs

Those are wise words to live by. Very wise. Use wisdom. If your dream is to backpack across Europe for a year without a job, well, that might not be the wisest dream to live out. But yet, if it's financially possible, go for it! Be responsible. Now, if you are debt free, and have a multimillion dollar money making idea, then by all means, *go for it*! Live your dreams. What are you waiting for?

The greatest gift you can give back to God is being who he created you to be. He was particular in what gifts he placed inside of you. The world awaits. Go seize and conquer.

This was totally the shortest chapter in the book. You're welcome. Everybody needs a break once in a while. You can take this extra time to go play outside today. Build a fort. Dig a tunnel. Catch grasshoppers. Re-live your elementary school days. You can thank me later.

A GREAT BIG
BEAUTIFUL TOMORROW

I have two favorite rides in Tomorowland at Walt Disney World's Magic Kingdom. I'm sure some of you would guess one of them to be Space Mountain. Nope. You're wrong. My husband and I were at Disney World last week for a Christian music conference. You know how those work, though, don't you? A few conference sessions. Play. A few more conference sessions. Play some more. And play we DID! We had a blast together. (And I guess it would be proper to mention that we did actually have some musical takeaways from the conference).

"Let's go on Space Mountain!" my cute

hubby suggested. Not my favorite. Trying to be a supportive wife, we got in line (a very short one thankfully), and boarded our pint-sized space rocket. I made sure that my 'security bar' was as tight as possible across my lap. As I braced myself for the upward ascent, I noticed all the teeny small children on the ride. *I really should be braver. Should, but I'm not.* I never have been a fan of roller coasters, although, *yes*, I realize this is a comparatively 'baby' roller coaster.

Relax I kept telling myself. *Re·lax. You're a grown woman. This ride is not going to injure you. Relax and try to enjoy this ride. Be a big girl.*

I didn't feel so horribly bad when, upon ascending to the top of the indoor coaster, we abruptly stopped short, and I heard my husband groan deeply when the security bar deeply jarred the insides of his lower abdomen. *See, I knew this ride was dangerous.*

I closed my eyes and braced my feet against the little foot rests in front of me. We twisted and turned, climbed and plummeted. And yes, I did make it out alive. Barely.

"I don't think I ever need to ride that again," I told my husband. He confided to me that his neck and back were hurting after that initial jolt we received. Whew. Of course I felt sorry for him, but I was also slightly relieved that I didn't have to 'journey to space' again. Now if in the future our grandchildren want to ride Space Mountain, I suppose I will have to put my 'big girl panties' on and pretend to enjoy it.

Now, you wanna know my *favorites*? I, yes I, am proud and not ashamed to admit that I love the People Mover. Granted, I realize that the People Mover really doesn't fall into the category of an official 'ride'. It's pretty much a monorail without a roof. But on a really hot day at Disney, you can enjoy some air conditioning and nice cool breezes up on the 'Mover'. It's relaxing. It's for old people. It's one of my favorites. Be nice.

My other favorite, you ask? Why, that would be one of the oldest and most famous Walt Disney-personally-created rides, the Carousel Of Progress. It. Is. Wonderful. It's another one of those not-have-to-wait-in-a-long-line rides. OK, well, again, this isn't necessarily a *ride,* although you do move in it. The audience moves *around* the stage. Pure genius.

An interesting fact about the Carousel Of Progress: It was created by Walt Disney for the GE (General Electric) Pavilion for the 1964-1965 World's Fair. I was conceived from two people that worked at the Kodak Pavilion for that same World's Fair. I'm thinking that perhaps while I was still but a wee zygote, my birth mother went on the Carousel Of Progress, and that is why I love the ride so deeply. I fell in love with that song while in utero. It all makes sense now.

A few years ago when we 'rode' The Carousel Of Progress, we had our two sons with us. We were on the very last scene. Do you remember it? The family is in the future, and Grandma is playing a video game. The scene is set at Christmas time. It's cute. I chuckled.

The song 'There's A Great Big Beautiful Tomorrow' played. The animatronic family sang along. The audience didn't move. We were supposed to have moved to the "please gather your things and depart from the ride" section. The animatronic family sang again. And again. The ride was stuck, and we were 'fortunate' to hear that wonderful song over and over again. Fun family memories. We still talk and laugh about it today.

Perhaps the ride is getting a tad old. It *is* two years older than I am, and I'm getting old myself. When my husband and I rode it last week, we were yet again blessed to have a 'double portion' of the great song during one scene. It was the scene where the wife is wallpapering the 'new' RUMPUS ROOM. It makes me smile just writing it now. Remember that scene? Remember the song? It's a classic, and since I knew I was going to write this chapter today, the song has been stuck in my head non-stop. That's OK. It's a great song with a great positive message.

Feel free to sing along, my friends. If you grew up going to Disney like I did, it should bring back special memories. OK, warm up those vocal chords. Mi-Mi-Mi-Mi-Mi. Ready, set, sing!

There's a great big beautiful tomorrow
Shining at the end of everyday
There's a great big beautiful tomorrow
And tomorrow's just a dream away

Man has a dream and that's the start
He follows his dream with mind and heart
And when it becomes a reality
It's a dream come true for you and me

So there's a great big beautiful tomorrow
Shining at the end of everyday
There's a great big beautiful tomorrow
Just a dream away

Are those not the best words ever? Well, to be honest, It's A Small World is a close second. Interestingly enough, both songs were written by the Sherman Brothers, who were good friends of Walt Disney. Just call me a walking book of Disney trivia. You're very welcome. I've got more if you want to contact me personally. Perhaps we could find all of the 'hidden Mickey's' around the Magic Kingdom and all the parks. Let's go!

"Fun song, Kirsten, but I'm still waiting for *my* dreams to come true. *My* dreams seem so very far away."

So what do you do in these middle times? You may be in junior high or high school, thinking 'I'm ready to be out on my own, living my dreams'. I tell high schoolers all the time that it's "all about that sheet of paper" (your diploma). Whatever it takes to graduate high school, do it! Suck it up. Make it through those tough teachers and classes that you don't like. Get that diploma in your hand. Stay out of trouble. Don't do stupid things that get you suspended. Be wise. Make good decisions. Because once you graduate, the world is yours.

I don't want you to think (especially at this point in the book) that I am saying life only begins after high school or college. There are just some necessary things you have to go through first. Like school. And getting the best grades you can. Unfortunately, needing good grades will open up doors for you that, if you're planning on attending college, you need opened.

I wasn't the straight A student. I did well, with A's, B's, and a few C's here and there. I was so heavily involved in the music and drama departments, that I honestly could have cared less about chemistry. I never use it as an adult. I didn't use it back in high school either. But I had to learn it, and get a passing grade, in order to go to college, and in order to study what I had a passion for.

When our sons entered college, their grades had a large impact on their financial assistance. Never going to use Advanced Placement/Honors Biology in your career? I understand. But what that high school class will do for you is open up financial and scholarship possibilities. When you have great financial assistance for college, you then have more freedom to go study what you love. It's a vehicle to get you to your dreams.

My husband sang and toured with a group called TRUTH. In its day, it was the number one touring Christian group. They had a song on one of their albums that I just loved called, Keep Believing. It's one of those encouraging songs, when you get down, and think that you're never going to reach your ultimate calling in life. The chorus to the song has these words:

Keep Believing
In what you know is true
Keep Believing
You know the Lord will see you through.

When troubles rise in your life

And you don't know what to do

You'll be fine

If you just

Keep Believing.

Those are great words. Even though you can't see what God is doing in your life at this very moment, keep holding on. Keep believing. Keep preparing.

Perhaps you feel that the Lord has planted a dream in your heart for your future. But that idea/vision seems so far off and unattainable. Perhaps it's because of your age, or lack of finances, or the environment in which you were born and live. Yet you know that you know God has revealed this life dream to you. What do you *do* in the meantime? You prepare.

I can remember how excited we were when we found out that we were pregnant with our first baby. We weren't making much money at the time, but we did our best to get everything we needed for our future newborn. We took the nine months to slowly store up all of our needed supplies. Each month we would buy a little more as we got the nursery set up.

We were living in Tulsa, Oklahoma at the time. I've always been quite the discount and thrifty shopper. It's my female form of game hunting. There's nothing like the Thrill of The Hunt—Thrift Store Edition. I love thrift stores. Especially really good ones that don't have that typical *scent.*

My husband and I found some great thrift stores in Tulsa, and were happily surprised to find such bountiful supplies of nearly-new baby clothes. To find baby clothes with the tags still on them in brand new condition? As if I, myself shot down the season's Trophy Elk. Yep, that wonderful.

We saw signs of an upcoming HALF-OFF sale. Now that's talking my language. Half-off of *thrift store* prices? Almost as delightful as a hot fudge brownie sundae. My husband (bless him for putting up with me) and I had our game plan. The thrift stores (there were two with the same half off sale that day) would open their doors at 7am. Our plan? To be the last ones in the store the night before.

Right before closing, we would take all the baby clothes that we wanted to purchase the next morning, and place them together in an obscure part of the store. (Be nice. We weren't making a lot of money back then, and we had to revert to extreme measures.) That way, when the doors opened in the morning, we were off to grab our loot, and be *outta there!*

We did it. We divided to conquer. We each had a vehicle. We each had a plan. We each had to accomplish the goal at hand. Run, grab, and buy.

You, my friend, would not believe the number of people that stood at those thrift store doors the next morning waiting to grab their discounted treasures. My goodness. And these people were determined. Thrift store door openings on ½ off days are not for the faint of heart. This was full·on battle mode. I had a mission. *YES, SIR. HOOAH!*

I used my pregnant state and mask of innocence to make it to the front of the line. Pregnant and sweet they all thought. Oh, if they only knew.

There he was. The manager was approaching the front door with the key. Wait. Wait. Calm down. Wait. And...*GO!* Still pregnant but innocent no more, I ran to my hidden loot. It was all there. The plan was succeeding. *Roger. Over and Out.*

I left all the innocents grazing through the racks. All the really cute newborn boy clothes were on their way outta there. Ya snooze ya lose. Mama bear was making sure that her baby cub would be dressed *fine.* Fine and on the cheap!

Sound impressive? My husband was an equal warrior. Two thrift store missions completed. Back and home in thirty minutes. Upon arriving back at our apartment, we dumped all our loot on the couch, and promptly counted up how much we had saved in our double quest. That was a *good* morning. That was wise preparation for our child.

Dave and I were doing what it took to get ready for our baby. You need to get ready for *your* 'baby'. You want your dream to come, right? Then start preparing for it as if it's already on its way.

Speak positive words, as if your ultimate calling and purpose is just around the corner. Be active in preparing for your vision to come alive. If we had just sat watching TV for the nine months prior to Tyler's birth, we could never have taken care of him! Our 'dream' would have arrived, but we wouldn't have known what to do, or how to take care of our newborn son.

I remember reading the book 'What To Expect When You're Expecting' (it's a book given to almost every expectant mother) as if it were my life support. I needed to soak up every last tidbit of information, so that I was as prepared as I could be to take care of a newborn child. Are you doing everything to prepare for your future? Perhaps God has your dream ready, but you haven't done your prep work. If God dropped your completed vision in your lap right now, would your dream die, because you haven't stored up your supplies?

I want you living in daily expectation. Believe that your future holds more than your past. Keep birthing new ideas, and preparing for their arrival. Know everything there is to know about the career field you dream about entering. Seek, find, and learn. Connect with those in your dream career now. Learn from them. How did they get to where there are now? What were the proper steps? Write every bit of information down. Read and re·read it all. Soak up every bit of knowledge you can. When it's time for God use you in your calling, your 'thank you' to him can be that you had done everything in your power to be worthy of what he has for you.

I believe in you. God believes in you. I believe you were created with amazing gifts and abilities. God *knows* you were created with amazing gifts and abilities.

Live your life full and fulfilled. Live everyday as if it were your last on Earth. Don't sit and wish for what never happened. Go out and seize the day. Check off every item on your bucket list. Make a difference in this world.

When you've lived every last second of your purpose here on Earth, and as you breathe your last breath, I pray that you will smile, and know that you *did* it. You lived the life God intended for you. You made it matter that you were here. Smile, relax, and move on to your next journey.

Someday I'll meet you there. We'll have all of eternity to chat. I would love for you to look me up. Let's get together. Then you can tell me all of your life's adventures, and how you lived every last second of your life full of anticipation for what God was going to do next.

We think there is so much for us to do here on Earth. We have no idea the plans and dreams God has ready for us in Heaven! This is just our rehearsal!

I WANT IT ALL
AND I WANT IT NOW!

I'm an old school woman. To an extent. Okay, I like old school music. A lot. And what generation doesn't like some good Queen. In my opinion, if you haven't learned the words to Bohemian Rhapsody by the time you graduate high school, you have failed at what's most important in life. I'm telling you now, knowing Bohemian Rhapsody lyrics are important. And if you don't sing along every time you hear the song...well...I just don't know if we can be friends.

Not everyone knows the lyrics to Queen's *I Want It All*. But most people will at least know the lines in the chorus that say, "I want it all, I want it all, I want it all, and I want it *now!*" (You have to scream the word 'now'. Trust me on this) If you have absolutely no idea what I'm referencing right now, you have disappointed me. Go look it up on YouTube. Listen to at least the chorus of the song, and then return back to reading this chapter.

Perhaps not a song sung during worship on Sunday mornings, but the chorus is slightly profound. We *do* want it all, and we *do* want it now. I do! Admitting this may make youth pastors across the country mad at me, but I'm just speaking honestly. I want all that God has for my life, and I would like it all immediately. Immediately plain to understand, and right in front of my face.

Why is waiting (and sometimes waiting a very long time) part of our life on this earth? We can get food immediately. We can get an answer to nearly any random question within seconds on the internet, but yet God makes us wait for certain events in our lives.

Most of you probably know the story of Moses. He was born an Israelite, but raised as an Egyptian in Pharaoh's house. He was given the best of the best, and raised as royalty. He killed a man, and fled to the desert for forty years. (His story starts in the book of Exodus, chapter one, and ends in

Deuteronomy chapter 34. It'll take you some time to get through it all, but well worth the read.) In those forty desert years, God used every single day of his seemingly non-important existence for when the day came for Moses to lead the country of Israel back *into the desert*. I'm sure Moses had days, weeks, months and years when he thought, "I want it all, and I want it now", but it never seemed to happen for him.

Finally, when Moses was eighty, God spoke to him through a burning bush, and told him that his time had finally come. It was his season to walk into the calling God had been preparing him for. Why forty years of waiting? Why did he have to shovel sheep dung for *forty years*? It was somehow God's perfect time of preparation, and exactly what Moses needed.

King David was anointed to be the next king of Israel when he was only a young teenager. He had to wait until he was thirty years old to actually become King. That's a lot of years to wait. Could you imagine *knowing* you were to be the next king, and then year after year...waiting? I'm sure there were many years when he would sing, "I want it all, I want it all, I want to be King, and I want it *NOW!*"

We are told in the book of Isaiah, "'For my thoughts are not your thoughts, neither are

your ways my ways,' declares the LORD."
God himself tells us (at least he let us in on
this knowledge a long time ago) that we can't
and don't think like he does. We have to
trust that he is doing everything in our best
interest. He wants to give us a hope and a
future (Joshua 29:11), but I don't really like
to wait a long time for that hope and future
to reveal itself.

A.) I want my personal life's mission to be
clear and exact.

B.) I want to impact the world and make a
difference ASAP!

So what *is* life's mission? To use every
single gift you have inside your mind, heart,
and body to show others who God is. It's a
way cool concept. God created us, our
giftings, talents, and desires to let others in
on his love for them.

I Corinthians chapter 12, starting at
verse 4 tells us, "God's various gifts are
handed out everywhere; but they all
originate in God's Spirit. God's various
ministries are carried out everywhere; but
they all originate in God's Spirit. God's
various expressions of power are in action
everywhere; but God himself is behind it all.
*Each person is given something to do that
shows who God is*: Everyone gets in on it,
everyone benefits."

Every single person on this planet is

given something to do! We're not here just to get a high school diploma, and find a random job. God wants us to thrive, and to use everything he put inside of us. He wants us to make a difference. That's our mission.

Why spend so much time in this book about what you're gifted at, and why you need to find out who you are? Because God desires to use those particular individual gifts! That's one of the way cool things about God. He doesn't just dump your aptitude for sports, or your artistic gifts simply for doing something fun (although it *is* fun!). You have a mission. You have the mission of showing other people Jesus in your life! When you can identify what you're good at, you can identify how God can use you. I don't want to sound all confusing.

What I got in trouble for in elementary school (talking too much) *was actually* a God-given gift. It took me years to realize that talking/communicating was my *thing*. Once I realized that it was what I loved to do, I found a way to *use* that gifting to communicate God's love to other people— *through speaking*.

Your gift (and if you've read this whole book, and still don't think you're good at anything—well—we might need to talk) is how God will communicate to others through you. Artists have different mediums (not the kind that predict the future), but a medium is the way an artist expresses him or herself. Different mediums are clay, acrylic paints, watercolors, drawing, metals, etc. One person may be more gifted at working with clay than acrylic paints. That's because God has given that person that specific gifting. Those that work with clay aren't better than watercolor users···it's just different.

Your mission to make a difference in this world is to know what your 'medium' is. How will God desire to work through you? How is he working through you right now? Because you don't have to wait until you have a college degree or years at a job to be making a difference. Right now, at this very moment in time, God wants to show his love to others by speaking through you! I think that's so cool. That is simply how you will 'matter' in this world.

Oh my gosh, if I had a dollar for every grown adult that still has no clue what their purpose on earth is, I'd be rich, and could retire in Hawaii. Even some parents don't have a clue as to what they're good at. Perhaps how *you* will impact your world is to encourage adults to find what their medium is! (I would listen to you!)

So...wanting it all, and wanting it *now* really isn't such a horrible thing after all. Why wouldn't we want to know all of our giftings, and how God wants to use us *right now*? TD Jakes is a pastor on TV. He's just way cool, and I love him. I heard him say this quote, and I want to share it with you.

"Your gifts don't always show up immediately. God uses your <u>experiences</u> to draw out of you skills and giftings you didn't even know you had."

Yes, get all the insight to the gifts you have right now in your life! Do it! But always live in expectation of never being bored with what God has placed inside of you···because you could have so much more yet to come!

Perhaps you are really good at pottery and clay, but you've never had the opportunity to try it! Just wait. God could have *so much more* for you in the coming years! This life ride isn't boring! Enjoy the journey. Make a difference. *Matter*.

Small Group Chapter Questions

Chapter one: MATTERING

What are humans here to accomplish? (I'll start off with an easy one. ☺)

Are animals placed on this earth for a mission? What's the difference between animals and humans in our purpose for being born?

If you could have been born in any other era of human history, when would you choose? Why? What would make it better than present day?

If you were born in a different country, do you think you would have turned out different, or would you basically be the same person?

Do you believe that all of your days are ordered by God, or is life more a random consequence of your choices?

If you're American, do you have more potential or importance than someone born on a remote island in a forgotten tribe of people?

Do you feel worthy of God using your life to show others who he is? How does one become worthy of that?

What does a person that 'has it all together' look like? What are their characteristics?

Define greatness. What makes a teenager 'great'?

What makes you unique? What traits do you have that set you apart?

Read Psalm 139, verses 1-4, 13-14, and 16. Do your best to verbally explain these verses to someone in kindergarten.

Just for fun:

--Would you rather live without music or TV?

--Would you rather be able to only whisper or only shout?

Chapter two: OLD SCHOOL

What do your parents do as their vocation? Do they seem to enjoy work? What about your grandparents? Was it hard work for them, or something they looked forward to?

How does your parent's view of work affect you in your view of careers and jobs? Does it inspire you? Make you view a job as something hard or enjoyable?

Have you ever sold products (Girl Scout cookies, etc.) as a child? Did/do you enjoy it? Were you rewarded for your hard work?

What is the worst thing you've had to sell? Your favorite thing to sell? Are you a natural 'salesman'?

How have your early views of having a job or career affected your current job (if you have one)?

Is a career more of a God-calling, or is it a vehicle to make money?

What product out in the market today could you improve on? Are you an ideas person that can always think of new and innovative products?

Do you know someone that gave up on their dreams? Why did they? Do you agree with their decision?

Can you identify experiences that have shaped you into the person you are today? Good experiences? Tough experiences?

Have you ever had what you thought was a great money making idea? What is it? How did you come up with the idea? Have you ever tried to make it work, as an actual product? Have other people (friends, family members, etc.) agreed that it was a great idea worth pursuing?

Just for fun:

--Would you rather have 500 tarantulas in your house, or 1000 crickets?
--Would you rather eat poison ivy, or a handful of bumblebees?

Chapter three: WHATCHYA WANNA BE?

If time, money, education and any other obstacle was a non-issue, what kind of work would you choose to do?

What did you always want to be when you were younger? Do you know what your parents wanted to be?

What were the dream jobs of your friends when you were little? If you're in a group right now, go around and have everyone share what they wanted to be when they were little.

Why do you think people choose different career paths than what they wanted to do when they were younger?

Do you know anyone that went on to be exactly what they said they were going to be?

Why do dream jobs change as we grow older?

Do you believe that your personal career calling was already mapped out for you by God while you were still in your mother's womb? If the answer is "yes", why do you think it takes so many of us so long to discover what we are meant to do?

If you could snap your fingers, and immediately invent your vocation, would you?

Name your top five abilities:

Name the top five areas of work that you're *not* good at:

What vocation would you *never* choose?

What is your dream for your future? Spell it out. Verbalize it. What is keeping you from attaining that dream? Time, relationships, finances, age?

Biblical predestination is the belief that God knows things ahead of time. The words translated "predestined" in the Scriptures referenced above are from the Greek word *proorizo*, which carries the meaning of "determine beforehand," "ordain," "to decide upon ahead of time." So, predestination is

God determining certain things to occur ahead of time. Here's my question to you: Do you think God has already determined (predestined) what career and jobs you are to have in your life, or is that a choice you make? Does it really matter what you do career-wise? Is that important to him?

Look up these verses about predestination: Ephesians 1:11, Acts 4:28, and Ephesians 1:5. Are these verses *only* about salvation, or do you think you can apply them to every area of your life?

Just for fun:

-- Would you rather run across a large vacant field containing 1000 angry rattlesnakes, or three land mines?
-- Would you rather marry the first person you see tomorrow, or never marry?

Chapter four: AIN'T NUTHIN' YOU CAN DO

Are you growing up in a positive environment?

Do you feel that the people you hang out with are verbally encouraging towards your gifts and abilities?? Are you verbally encouraging to your friends?

Can you see the effects of your environmental upbringing in your life today? (Either positive or negative)

Are the words your parents are speaking to you today influencing the career path you want?

Do you come from a line of successful people? Define successful. Define unsuccessful.

Are your parents steering you into a particular career? Do you feel forced to follow in their footsteps, and obey their wishes for your vocation?

The Bible tells us to honor our parents. If you feel the strong desire to go into the medical field, yet your parents are wanting you to do something completely different, are you 'dishonoring' them by going into the medical field? How does one still honor their parents, but yet choose a different career path?

Have you ever felt like you don't have any

talent? Why do you believe you have felt that way? How can a person change that mindset?

Dig a bit in your Bible. What does God say about who you are? Look up these verses:

Jeremiah 29:11

John 1:12

Galatians 3:26

I Peter 2:10

Ephesians 3:16-19

Jeremiah 31:3

Zephaniah 3:17

I John 3:1

**Keep these positive reminders in your heart.

Just for fun:

··Would you rather end hunger or end hatred?
··Would you rather lose your legs, or lose your arms?

Chapter five: SECRET

INGREDIENT

Do you like to cook or bake? Just cook? Just bake? What's the difference between cooking and baking?

What do you enjoy making (or eating) over and over again? What food could you easily eat every single day of your life?

What do you *love to do*?

What is your passion? What things are you passionate about?

What are you naturally good at?

Do you know people who think they are literally 'good at nothing'? How does that thinking coincide with God's word?

When you read this chapter, did you come up with a list of 'things you are good at'? Verbally share your top five.

What fills your thoughts in the quiet moments when you're riding the bus, driving, or lying in bed? What do you think about incessantly, what captures your imagination? Politics? Spirituality? Relationships?

What aspects of your current job (if you have one) do you love? Which do you loathe?

What activity makes you completely lose track of time, because you are completely enjoying it?

Did you ask your friends what they thought you were good at? What did they say? Ask your small group friends the same question.

What have you secretly dreamed of doing with your life?

Just for fun:

-- Would you rather be invisible, or read minds?
-- Would you rather be 3 ft. tall, or 9 ft. tall?
-- Would you rather have a boring repetitive job that paid $90,000/year or and engaging job that you really enjoy, but it pays $45,000/year?

Chapter 6: MR. & MRS. DOWNER

Are your friends on the whole, very upbeat and positive, or slightly depressing.

What kind of people do you usually hang around with?

Do you have a lot of friends, or are they a small circle? What qualities do your closest friends have?

When was the last time you were intellectually challenged by your friends? Spiritually challenged?

Is there someone in your life that always cuts you down, and you always feel horrible after you spend time with them? Why are they still your friend (or is it a relative?)?

Do you feel an obligation to be around certain people, even though you know that spiritually and emotionally, they're not good for you?

If you became a Christian recently, did you keep the same friends? Were your non-Christian friends still influential in your life? Were you made fun of for becoming a Christian, or did they support your decision?

Who do you need to filter from being an influence in your life? Can you? Is that too difficult to do?

Have you ever made the decision to distance yourself from someone that was a negative influence in your life? How did they react? Did the friendship continue? How did you *do* the 'distancing'? What would you recommend to someone that needs to distance themselves from this type of person?

Just for fun:

--Would you rather eat a bar or soap, or a bottle of dishwashing liquid?
--Would you rather find true love or 10 million dollars?

Chapter seven:

THE PRINCIPAL'S OFFICE

Can you name the names of your elementary, junior high, or high school principals? Did you have/are you having a good relationship with your principals?

Who was the meanest teacher you ever had? Were they mean to everyone, or just you? Why do you think they were that way?

(If) you got in trouble when you were younger, what would you usually get in trouble for? Has that 'trouble making' quality turned out to be a strength of yours?

What is your 'identity' in junior high or high

school? The funny one? Loud one? Quiet one? Smart one? Artistic one? Athletic one? Trouble maker? Popular one? What are you involved in? Sports, theater, band, choir, FFA, academic clubs, student government, home economics?

Have you transformed from your elementary or junior high identity? Changed? Stayed the same?

Did other people label you as a certain type of student, but deep down you knew you weren't that type of person? If so, how did you break out of that stereotype?

Just for fun:

-- Would you rather be a dog's chew toy, or a cat's litter box?
-- Would you rather lose your sense of taste and smell, or lose your ability to distinguish colors?

Chapter eight: DUES

On a scale of 1-10 (ten being really patient), how naturally patient are you? Are you more patient as a Christian believer? Does that help in the 'I want it instantly' situations?

What are you currently waiting for in your life?

What do you want to do, but it seems to be taking so long, you are considering giving it up?

Have you ever seen someone give up on their dreams because the process was too long or difficult? How did their life change, once they gave up? Have you ever given up on something (or someone) because the process was too long?

Do you currently have someone in your life who is *where* you want to be? They are what/who *your* goal is, but you aren't there yet. Are they willing to help and mentor you?

Never burn bridges. How does this statement apply to your life? Are there bridges you have burnt that you now regret? Why did you burn the bridge? Out of anger? Hurt? If you could go back and re-live that situation, what would you change? *Would* you change anything?

Moses was 80 when he was reinvented to be the leader of Israel. If you could live until the age of 120, what would your life look like? What would you want to accomplish in 120 years? Verbally 'map it out'.

Do you have a dream business? Is it exactly what you're doing right now? If you could snap your fingers and be in your perfect job scenario, what would it be? What would the name of your company be? Why *that* name?

Do you have a great money making idea that hasn't been created yet? What is it? What is holding you back from creating and selling it (if it's an actual product)? What about your spouse? What is one of their great 'we could retire from that money' idea?

Do you consider yourself a creative person? Do you daily realize that your creative ideas come from God himself, who is the ultimate creator?

If money weren't an option, what product, or business would you create?

Just for fun:

··Would you rather drink a bowl full of gravy, or have a large spider stuck in your hair?
··Would you rather have one wish granted today, or three wishes granted in ten years?

Chapter 8.5: APPLE SLICE

Define intuition without looking it up.

Now look up the word intuition. Is the 'official' definition different than what you originally thought?

Is there a difference between intuition and God speaking to you? How do you know when/if the Holy Spirit is speaking to you?

Have you had positive responses from people about what you feel is your gifting/purpose?

Have family members and loved ones

affirmed your giftings and callings?

Do you know anyone that has 'checked out' of normal life to pursue an unrealistic dream? Where are they now? How did their actions affect their family?

Have you struggled and struggled to make your own (current life's) dream come true, but you're still waiting? Why do you think this is happening? What do you need to change or adjust, or give up in your life?

Are you grateful for this short chapter?

Just for fun:

--Would you rather give up your computer, or
   your beloved pet?
--Would you rather have a lifetime supply of
   meals from your favorite restaurant, or a
   lifetime supply of gasoline for your car?

Chapter nine: A GREAT BIG BEAUTIFUL TOMORROW

What is your favorite ride at Disney? Why? Do you have any favorite Disney memories?

What dream are you currently waiting for in your life to come true?

How would you like your life to turn out? What do you think are the steps to getting there?

How would you change your day today, if you knew the dream you have been waiting for would be fulfilled tomorrow? *Would* you change anything?

If you knew the dream, vision, or mission God gave you was literally just around the corner, how would you prepare? What still needs to be done? What things in your life would you delete? What would you keep the same?

Who have you connected with that is already doing what you want to be doing? Are you in an apprentice-type relationship with them? Do you currently mentor anyone that wants to be involved in *your* job?

When God gives us a mission for our lives, it's for a greater purpose. Have you been able to witness and understand what God's mission is so far for your life? Can you share how you know that's why you've been put on this earth?

When I die, I want God to tell me, I lived every day full of purpose, and that I fulfilled my mission and purpose on earth. What is burning inside of your soul, that you feel you have to accomplish while alive in this world?

Just for fun:

··Would you rather live one 1000-year life, or ten 100-year lives?
··Would you rather have a head the size of a tennis ball or the size of a watermelon?

Chapter ten: I WANT IT ALL AND
I WANT IT NOW

If you knew that in twenty years, you would have all the wealth and prominence you could ever want, could you patiently wait out 7,300 days? Would you need to attain that in less days? Are you patient by nature? Does patience come easily to you, or do you want immediate results?

Have you ever felt that God told you to do something for someone, or to say something to someone, but you were afraid to do it? Why do you think you felt that way? How can a person know it's actually God speaking to them, and not just a random thought?

If your 'gifts don't always show up immediately' saying is true, would you be willing to wait out additional talents and gifts in your life? What if those gifts are results of pain? What *wouldn't* you be willing to go through to have more skills come about in your life?

Read Isaiah 40, verse 31. How does that verse make you feel? Have you ever seen a real eagle soar? Now go back and read verse 30 of that same chapter. They are contrasting verses. Verse 30 tells us that on our own, we can get weary (even you *young* people!). The contrast? If/when we wait upon the *Lord*, there is a vast difference. How does a person 'wait upon the Lord'? What does that mean?

Have you ever been promised something, and had to wait a long time for it? What was it? How long do you have until you graduate high school? Calculate how many actual days you have until you graduate. How will you cope until that day? What gives you the stamina to make it through those days?

Have you gained any insight into your life from reading this book? (I am really hoping there is *something* you learned) What words would you tell a friend who is feeling like they have no purpose for being alive? What are some of your favorite encouraging Bible verses? When you are having a discouraging day, how do you rise about those feelings?

Have you learned or listened to the chorus of Queen's 'I Want It All' song yet? ☺

Just for fun:

--Would you rather have legs as long as your fingers, or fingers as long as your legs?
--Would you rather visit 100 years in the past, or 100 years in the future?
--Would you rather be able to fly or be able to breathe under water?
--Would you rather read my book ten more times, or have to take College Algebra every year for the rest of your life? (THAT BETTER BE AN EASY ONE TO

ANSWER!)

Queen Esther was just an ordinary Hebrew girl that God reinvented into a Queen in order to save His people. King David was reinvented from a shepherd boy to a King. Moses was 80 when he was called to lead the nation of Israel.

What does God have yet in store for your life? Explore the possibilities that God has for you in every changing season of your journey.

Newlywed to young mom to empty nester to retirement age--God can transform your life at every stage to use your gifts in ways greater than you could ever imagine. There are no limits to how God can reinvent your life to maximize all of your potential.

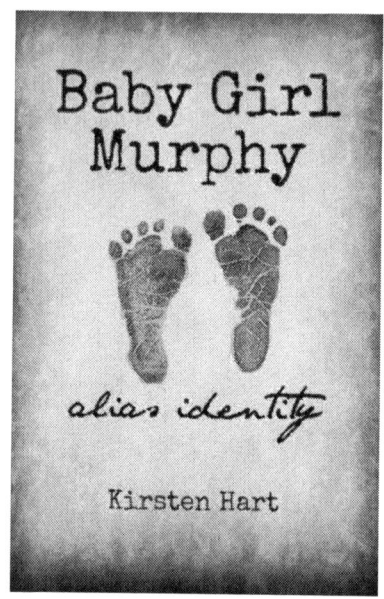

"I'm sorry, Mrs. Hart, we don't have any birth records for you." These were the words I heard over the phone when I was trying to locate a copy of my birth certificate for a new passport. "Have you checked with the Adoption Registry Office?" was the following question. Adoption? I was forty-one years old. I knew who my parents were. Why would someone suggest that I talk with an Adoption Registry Office? I just simply needed a copy of my birth certificate. That phone call led me on a new journey of discovery and secrets.

Who was I? Who was my birth mother? Did I have other siblings? What was my story? Baby Girl Murphy is my personal exploration of discovering my new identity and unveiling a secret that God had kept for 41 years. A secret so dear, yet so mysterious. "...Find out more..." were the words I kept hearing echo through my heart. Indeed I did find out more. More than I ever dreamed imaginable.

WWW.AMAZON.COM

CHAT is for every small group that enjoys digging into intriguing Biblical topics. Set aside time to grab some snacks and coffee, and journey into a Bible study that seeks to draw out conversations whether in a living room or neighborhood café.

This is not your average small group study. CHAT contains twelve individual topics that aren't successive, yet can be used on a weekly basis. Pick and choose. Jump around. It's up to you.

Designed for busy people with an appetite for truth, and connection with each other and God.

WWW.AMAZON.COM

CHAT is for every teen group that enjoys digging into intriguing Biblical topics. Set aside time to grab some snacks and a cappuccino, and journey into a Bible study that seeks to draw out conversations whether in a living room or neighborhood café.

This is not your average small group study. CHAT contains twelve individual topics that aren't successive, yet can be used on a weekly basis. Pick and choose. Jump around. It's up to you. Designed for busy teens with an appetite for truth, and connection with each other and God.

*CHAT Teens is the teen version of CHAT for adults—(the red cup cover). CHAT Teens contains the same chapter topics as the adult version (except for one chapter) just worded for the teen audience. Teens and their parents can dig in, and discuss the same Bible topics at home!

WWW.AMAZON.COM

CHAT Christmas is a special edition of the CHAT 'A Conversational Bible Study' series. Usually the CHAT books contain twelve separate chapters. This Christmas edition only contains four, and is meant as a special study to fit in-between Thanksgiving and Christmas. Designed to concentrate on this time of celebrating Thanksgiving and the birth of our Lord.

CHAT was designed not to be a right or wrong answer conversational Bible study. No questions to fill in. And if you miss a week, you can't get behind. Every week has a non-chronological different topic of discussion. Grab a cup of coffee, a snack, and dig into challenging topics with your small group.

ABOUT THE AUTHOR

Why hire you as a speaker?
Because I can hula-hoop, and I think when people fall, it's *always* funny.

What makes you different as a speaker?
I can hula-hoop.

Are you too old to be a youth speaker?
No. Age is in your mind. Mind-wise, I fit well in junior high.

What is your favorite food?
Yes.

What makes you stand out as a speaker?
I accidentally found out (as an *adult!*) I had been adopted, and my parents never told me. That's not too common.

What is your best camp prank?
I was a senior high camp counselor for our church's youth camp. I had someone steal a pair of underwear from one of our popular teen boys. I melted a Hershey's kiss, and smeared it all over the inside of the underwear, wrote his name on the 'band' with a large sharpie, and placed it on the sidewalk on the way to the cafeteria.

What is your favorite sport?

What's a sport? Actually, I just recently kayaked through an alligator-infested creek in Florida, and I think that's my new 'thing'. Plus, I can play some mean shuffleboard.

What is your spiritual heartbeat?

My desire is that teens will have a thirst and desire to dig deep into the Word of God to understand *why* they believe *what* they believe. God created all of us for a specific mission while alive on this planet, and if I can help guide teens towards that purpose and mission, I feel fulfilled.

Made in the USA
Charleston, SC
29 June 2016